THE FULL TREATMENT

A Comedy in Three Acts

by

MICHAEL BRETT

SAMUEL FRENCH

LONDON
NEW YORK TORONTO SYDNEY HOLLYWOOD

MADE AND PRINTED IN GREAT BRITAIN BY
LATIMER TREND AND CO. LTD, WHITSTABLE
MADE IN ENGLAND

THE FULL TREATMENT

Produced by The Devonshire Park Theatre Company, at the Devonshire Park Theatre, Eastbourne, on the 15th February 1966, with the following cast of characters:

(in order of their appearance)

GEORGE MAXWELL, a reporter	*Richard Saire*
BRENDA MAXWELL, his wife	*Dinah Handley*
SUSAN, an hotel maid	*Carole Carter*
STELLA HALEY, a secretary	*Janice Hosker*
JOAN BANSTEAD, a photographer	*Christine Edmonds*
PHILIP SCOTT, a public relations officer	*Geoffrey Lea*
FREDERICK ELTON, an editor	*Oliver Fisher*
HENRY MELLOWES, a celebrity	*Clarkson Rose*
SARAH MELLOWES, his wife	*Peggy Paige*
ELIZABETH WELLING, a nurse	*Mary Gauntlett*
GEOFFREY WALLCOT-BROWN, a B.B.C. interviewer.*	*Richard Vanstone*

Produced by RICHARD BURNETT
Setting by NEVILLE USHER

SYNOPSIS OF SCENES

The action of the play passes in the sitting-room of the penthouse suit of the Royal Park Hotel, London

ACT I

Early afternoon of a spring day

ACT II

The following morning

ACT III

SCENE 1 About 10 p.m. the same evening
SCENE 2 About 7 p.m. the following evening

Time—the present

* If desired this character can be a girl

ACT I

SCENE—*The sitting-room of the penthouse suite of the Royal Park Hotel,*
London. Early afternoon of a spring day.
   There are double entrance doors RC, *opening on to a passage. A door*
down L *leads to the principal bedroom and a door up* R *leads to a second*
bedroom. There is a large window with a window-seat up LC *with a view*
over London. A built-in, fully equipped bar is in an alcove up C. *The room*
is elegantly furnished in modern style. A desk with a telephone is against the
wall down R, *with an upright chair* L *of it. Tall pedestals, with vases of*
flowers on them, stands up R *and up* L. *An occasional table is* L. *A sofa is*
LC *and two armchairs stand* RC *with an occasional table between them. A*
long stool is in front of the bar, and there are shelves for bottles and glasses
on the wall behind the bar. On the walls up C *and* L *are good, modern*
paintings. At night, the room is lit by wall-brackets R *and* L *in the alcove*
up C, *and a table-lamp on the table* L. *The light switch is* L *of the double*
doors. In the passage, there is a console table with a vase of flowers on it.
In any other suitable way, it may be indicated that this is the best room in
a luxury hotel.

When the CURTAIN *rises, the room is empty.*

SUSAN (*off*) If you'd kindly follow me, sir. This way.

   (SUSAN *enters by the double doors and stands* L *of them. She is an hotel*
maid, and is young and neat, and very correct.
      GEORGE *and* BRENDA MAXWELL *follow Susan on,* BRENDA *lead-*
ing. GEORGE, *a reporter, is in his middle twenties. He is youthfully hand-*
some with a lithe body and quick of movement. He is well-dressed, with a
flower in his buttonhole. Ordinarily, he radiates an infectious gaiety, but
at present he is slightly ill-at-ease. BRENDA *is aged about thirty, elegantly*
dressed and worldly. She has a hard beauty which owes much to expensive
treatments. BRENDA *stands up* C. GEORGE *is* R *of Brenda*)

Here you are, sir. Our penthouse suite. Everything's prepared for
you.
GEORGE. Thank you.
SUSAN. This is the sitting-room. (*She crosses to the door down* L) Over
here is the principal bedroom.
GEORGE. Oh—er—later, if you wouldn't mind.
SUSAN. Certainly, sir. (*She moves to* L *of Brenda*) The bathroom is
en suite—the main bathroom, that is.
GEORGE. Thank you very much.

   (SUSAN *crosses to the double doors.* GEORGE *gives her a coin*)

SUSAN. Thank you. sir. I'll have your luggage put into your room right away.

GEORGE. It's very kind of you.

SUSAN. Just telephone if you need anything.

GEORGE. Right.

(SUSAN *exits by the double doors*)

BRENDA. George, you can't mean we're spending our honeymoon here?

GEORGE. Didn't I say I had a surprise for you? This is it. (*With a wave of his hand*) The famous penthouse suite. Haunt of film stars, royalty, American millionaires, world statesmen, the lot. Cary Grant was here last week.

BRENDA. But how? I know we were married this morning for better or for worse; but how did it suddenly get this much better? (*She moves to the door down* L. *opens it and looks off*)

GEORGE (*moving down* C) Three days here, then off to Italy as we planned. Isn't it marvellous?

BRENDA (*closing the door*) Miraculous is the word I'd use. I mean— (*she moves to* L *of the sofa*) I dare say you're a good reporter but the *County Gazette* can't pay this kind of salary. Or are we honeymooning now and paying later?

GEORGE. No, no, nothing like that. Matter of fact, it's a present. From my editor. You know—Mr Elton.

BRENDA. Mr Elton!

GEORGE (*moving below the right end of the sofa*) Decent of him, don't you think?

BRENDA (*moving to* L *of George*) Yes, especially as you're always telling me he's meaner than a paranoic tax-collector.

GEORGE. Well, he is normally. Fact is he was rather taken with a story I turned in recently. (*He moves* C) Anyway, what are we standing here arguing about? Aren't you pleased?

BRENDA. Darling, of course I'm pleased. (*She moves to* L *of George*) When did you know about it?

GEORGE. Only this morning.

BRENDA. I must have a look around. (*She crosses to the door* R, *opens it and looks off*) How many rooms are there?

GEORGE (*moving to the window*) This room, five bedrooms and three bathrooms.

BRENDA (*closing the door*) Five bedrooms! Isn't that rather excessive—even for a honeymoon? (*She crosses to George*) Darling, you're very sweet and I adore you when you look embarrassed. (*She hugs him*) I really believe that's why I married you. I don't know what it is. You make me feel a young girl again. Not, of course, that I'm much more. (*She holds George's face with both hands and kisses him*) We're going to be deliriously happy, aren't we?

GEORGE. Yes, of course.

BRENDA. You don't sound all that sure, dear. Is anything bothering you?

GEORGE. Good Lord, no.

BRENDA. Then that's all right. (*She turns to the bar*) Oh, look at all the lovely booze. Another present from your editor?

GEORGE. Yes.

BRENDA (*removing her hat and coat*) Then let's have some. Any champagne there? (*She puts her hat and coat on the window-seat*)

GEORGE (*moving behind the bar*) I'll see. (*He looks at the bottles*) No. Everything else. Gin, whisky, sherry, vodka . . .

BRENDA. Gin. You have a whisky, darling. A good stiff one.

GEORGE. No, too early.

BRENDA. Nonsense! It'll pull you together.

GEORGE. There's nothing wrong with me. (*He pours drinks*)

BRENDA (*admiringly*) That's my opinion, too. (*She sits on the sofa at the left end of it*) I'm expecting great things of you, darling.

(GEORGE'S *hand shakes and the bottle rattles against the glass*)

There you go again. Oh, well, I suppose it's natural you should be on edge after all that fuss and bother of the wedding, this morning, especially that very sexy address we got from the vicar. It wasn't so bad for me, having been through it all before. Bring them over here.

(GEORGE *brings the drinks to the sofa, then sits* R *of Brenda on it*)

(*She takes her drink*) Thank you, dear. What a relief to be alone at last. (*She raises her glass*) To us.

(*They kiss gently, then drink*)

I must say I'm surprised your paper can afford all this. Didn't you say it was on its last legs?

GEORGE. No. I said it was losing money.

BRENDA. Isn't that the same thing?

GEORGE. No, because the owner, Miss Jessop, doesn't run it for money.

BRENDA. What does she run it for? Oh, you told me. As a memorial to her father, who founded it. Good for her. We'll drink to her. (*She raises her glass*) Miss Jessop.

(*They drink*)

How much longer are they going to be with our luggage?

GEORGE. It may be in our room. They'd take it straight in from the corridor.

BRENDA. Then have a look, will you, dear?

GEORGE. Of course. (*He rises and moves to the door* R)

BRENDA. Not that room, George. (*She points* L) This one.

GEORGE. Oh, Lord, yes. (*He moves to the bar and puts down his glass*)

(BRENDA *snuggles back with arms raised*)

BRENDA. Oh, I'm going to be so happy with you, George. I'm only now beginning to live. You feel that, too?

GEORGE (*crossing to the door* L) Yes, yes, I do.

(GEORGE *exits* L, *leaving the door open*)

BRENDA. I never once felt like this with my first husband. Though, of course, he was a great deal older than me, poor man.

(GEORGE *enters* L *and stands* L *of the sofa*)

GEORGE. No, not there yet.

BRENDA. Why not? Call this service! I bet they didn't treat Cary Grant like this. Ring down.

GEORGE. Brenda, there's something you ought to know.

BRENDA. Really? Well, if it's a belated pre-marital confession, I don't want to hear it. Start that, and there's no knowing where we'll finish up.

GEORGE. Brenda, please.

BRENDA. George, dear. I don't know what you're going to tell me, but provided you haven't married me bigamously, or anything like that, and are in possession of all your faculties . . . (*She rises and hands George her glass*) Good God, it isn't that, is it?

GEORGE (*putting the glass on the table* L) Certainly not.

BRENDA. For a moment . . .

GEORGE (*turning to her*) Brenda!

BRENDA. Sorry, dear. (*She sits on the sofa, at the right end of it*) Do go on.

GEORGE (*sitting* L *of Brenda on the sofa*) You never read the *County Gazette,* do you?

BRENDA. Does anyone? Honestly, George, the sooner you pack it up and return to London the better. What's the use of my owning two businesses, if my own husband insists on being an ill-paid reporter on some ghastly provincial newspaper that's going downhill, anyway?

GEORGE. I've no intention of living on the businesses your husband left you.

BRENDA. But that's silly.

GEORGE. Brenda, we've been all over that.

BRENDA. I'm sure the managers are swindling me. I'd much rather you swindled me.

GEORGE (*rising*) Do you want to hear or not?

BRENDA. But, of course, my sweet.

GEORGE. Then listen. (*He crosses to* RC) I've told you about Miss Jessop.

BRENDA. The elderly spinster who owns your newspaper. What about her?

GEORGE (*turning*) Miss Jessop is very keen on marriage.

BRENDA. Me too, darling.

GEORGE. Marriage as an institution, I mean. She belongs to

societies that foster it, look after girls with babies, find them husbands, that sort of thing.

BRENDA. Sounds like a full-time job.

GEORGE (*crossing to* R *of the sofa*) Anyway, that's why she was so
delighted with the story I wrote.

BRENDA. Which story?

GEORGE. The one that got us this suite as a present. I told you
about it.

BRENDA. You mean about that old couple you found in some
village? They were both a hundred years old, weren't they?

GEORGE. Yes, and on Saturday they'll have been married for
eighty years.

BRENDA. How perfectly wonderful! Do give them my congratulations.

GEORGE. Oh, I will. (*He moves up* RC) The moment they arrive.

BRENDA. The moment they what?

GEORGE (*turning*) They're coming here to celebrate.

BRENDA. This hotel, you mean?

GEORGE. Well, actually—this suite.

BRENDA (*rising*) What!

GEORGE. I have to cover the story.

BRENDA (*moving down* L) Just a minute . . . (*She turns*)

GEORGE (*moving to* R *of the sofa*) You see, I mentioned in my
story that the old lady longed to come to London just once before
she died. Well, our readers got up a fund.

BRENDA (*moving to* L *of the sofa*) Are you telling me I'm honeymooning with you and two centenarians?

GEORGE. Oh, they won't be any bother. There'll be a trained
nurse with them.

BRENDA. A trained nurse! (*She moves to the window and turns*) It
gets better all the time. You must be mad.

GEORGE (*moving to her*) But, Brenda . . .

BRENDA (*turning to face him*) Or were you thinking of turning in
with the trained nurse while I sing the old people to sleep?

GEORGE. Darling, I realize how you feel but it needn't make
any difference to us. Mr Elton's secretary will be here to see to all
the arrangements.

BRENDA. A secretary, too. Who else?

GEORGE. No-one. Well, except a photographer.

BRENDA. A photographer! Are you daring to stand there and tell
me I'm spending my honeymoon with two centenarians, a trained
nurse, a secretary and a photographer? (*She moves down* L) What
about your editor? Isn't he coming?

GEORGE (*following Brenda down* L) As a matter of fact, he is.

BRENDA. Oh! (*She crosses to* C)

GEORGE (*following to* L *of Brenda*) Only this afternoon. Just to
welcome them.

BRENDA (*moving* RC) I don't believe it. It isn't true. It can't be.

GEORGE (*moving* c) I'm terribly sorry. We'd arrange for someone else to cover the story—a fellow called "Peters"—only the old couple refused to come with him—insisted on me. You know how cantankerous the very old can be. Well, we couldn't drop the story. Our readers have put up the money. They're expecting full coverage.

BRENDA (*sitting in the armchair* RC) How can you do this to me? How can you even think of it?

GEORGE (*moving to* L *of her*) Brenda, please . . .

BRENDA (*rising*) I won't have it.

(BRENDA *moves towards* GEORGE *who backs below the sofa*)

(*She follows George*) You can ring whoever it is and tell them if those two aged lovebirds enter this room I'll hurl them both down the nearest staircase. I'd never have believed it possible. You're supposed to love me. We were only married this morning.

GEORGE. But it's only for three days.

BRENDA. I don't care if it's only three hours. They're not coming here. (*She moves up* c)

GEORGE. I can't stop them now. (*He moves to* L *of Brenda*) They're on the way.

BRENDA (*crossing below George to the window-seat*) Then we'll go to another hotel—or to my flat. (*She picks up her hat and coat*)

GEORGE. Your flat? I thought you'd given it up.

BRENDA. I changed my mind. We might need it. We can't spend our whole lives in East Anglia. Anyway, that's beside the point. Well, what's it to be—another hotel or the flat?

GEORGE. I gave Mr Elton my word.

BRENDA. I'll give him a piece of my mind.

GEORGE. You can't do that.

BRENDA. Can't I? (*She sits on the left arm of the sofa*) I'm not afraid of him if you are. Well, you can take your choice. It's them or me. I mean it.

GEORGE (*leaning over the back of the sofa*) I'll need time to tell someone.

BRENDA. So long as you do it. My God, I've heard of some strange honeymoons but this beats the lot.

(*There is a knock at the double doors*)

GEORGE. Oh, Lord—(*he moves towards the double doors*) that'll be the secretary.

BRENDA. I can't believe it. I still can't believe it.

GEORGE. Brenda, listen. (*He turns and moves below the right end of the sofa*) I realize how you feel but this is the biggest story Mr Elton has ever let me handle. It's important to me.

BRENDA (*rising*) More important than your marriage to me?

GEORGE. No, of course not. But it's only for three days. We were spending three days in town in any case.

(*There is a knock at the double doors*)

(*He calls*) Just a minute. What about it, Brenda?

BRENDA. Have you no sense of proportion? (*She moves to L of George*) Well, of course, you haven't. It's because you do such mad things that I was attracted to you in the first place, God help me.

GEORGE. Then couldn't you . . . ?

BRENDA. But this is too much. I don't find your craziness quite so charming when it hits me.

(*There is a knock at the double doors*)

Get rid of her. Which is supposed to be our room?

GEORGE (*indicating the door* R) That one.

BRENDA. You're sure? (*She crosses to the door* R) Or were we going to be parked in an attic somewhere? I'll be in there while you're getting yourself out of this ridiculous mess. And mind you do it, George. I know marriages tend to grow shorter nowadays but this one could easily be a record for brevity.

(BRENDA *exits* R. *There is a knock at the double doors*)

GEORGE (*calling*) Come in. (*He flops on to the sofa, at the right end of it*)

(STELLA HALEY *enters by the double doors. She is aged about twenty-five, pretty and capable but unsophisticated. She wears a business-like but stylish suit and hat, and carries a brief-case and a portable typewriter. She moves to* R *of the sofa*)

STELLA. Well, George, have you told her? I see you have. What happened? (*She puts the case and typewriter on the bar, removes her hat and coat and puts them on the window-seat*)

GEORGE. We're leaving.

STELLA. I can't say I blame her. (*She looks towards the door* R) In there.

GEORGE. Yes.

STELLA. Who's going to tell our esteemed but apoplectic editor?

GEORGE. I thought you might.

STELLA. No, thanks.

GEORGE. But, Stella . . .

STELLA. Not me. (*She collects the typewriter, crosses and puts in on the desk*) You forget that without you the whole thing's off. They refuse to come. Evidently you made a big hit with them. (*She sets up the typewriter ready for use*)

GEORGE. Rubbish! I didn't even see . . . (*He breaks off*)

STELLA. What?

GEORGE (*rising*) Nothing.

STELLA. You started to say . . .

GEORGE. It wasn't important.

STELLA. I know you. You're hiding something. (*She moves* RC) Oh, no!

GEORGE. Now, see here, Stella, I've got enough on my plate . . .

STELLA (*moving* C) That day you wrote up the old couple—did you actually see them?

GEORGE (*moving down* L) You read my story.

STELLA. Did you?

GEORGE. The old man but not her. (*He sits on the left arm of the sofa*) She'd gone to bed.

STELLA. But you described her—her sweet, lined old face, her tranquil air, her quick sense of humour . . . What about that moving passage about her longing to see London once before she died?

GEORGE. Oh, that. I thought it up on the way back to the office.

STELLA. But our readers have flooded us with money to make it come true.

GEORGE. You don't have to tell me.

STELLA. You must be out of your mind. (*She moves below the right end of the sofa*) What if the *Courier* gets hold of this?

GEORGE. That rag!

STELLA. That rag, as you call it, is our biggest rival. They even want to take us over. They'd jump at the chance of showing us up as phoneys.

GEORGE. How can they do that?

STELLA. How? (*She moves up* C *and turns, then stands behind the sofa*) On second thoughts, George, you'd better explain the situation to your wife and persuade her to let you stay and cover the story.

GEORGE (*looking away*) She won't.

STELLA (*crossing down* L *and turning to face George*) She'd better. Mr Elton's built this into a big thing. If something goes wrong with it, you'll be out on your ear. I mean it, George.

GEORGE. Well, I'll speak to her. (*He rises and crosses to* C) But it won't do any good.

STELLA. Do it now. (*She moves below the sofa*) They'll all be here soon.

GEORGE (*moving to the door* R) I doubt if she'll even listen. Fine wedding day, this. Four hours since the ceremony and we've already had our first row.

(GEORGE *taps on the door* R *and exits.* STELLA, *with a shake of her head, moves to the bar and opens her brief-case*)

JOAN (*off; calling*) Stella! Stella!

STELLA (*calling*) In here.

(JOAN BANSTEAD *enters by the double doors. She is about twenty-eight, attractive and sophisticated. She wears outdoor clothes. Slung around her neck is a camera fitted with a flash*)

JOAN (*moving to* R *of Stella*) Ah, there you are.

STELLA. Joan, what are you doing up here? You'll miss them when they arrive.

JOAN. I'm seeking refuge—from the hotel P.R.O. You want to watch him, Stella. He has telescopic arms.

STELLA. One of those, is he?

JOAN. Jet-propelled. (*She crosses below Stella to the window*) Where's the happy couple?

(STELLA *beckons for silence and points towards the door* R)

STELLA. He's trying to talk her round.

JOAN. I'll bet she's giving him hell. Still, it's best for a marriage to start off as it's likely to continue. What do you think of her?

STELLA (*picking up her brief-case and moving to the desk*) From just that glimpse of her at the wedding, she seemed very nice. (*She sits at the desk*)

JOAN. You think everyone's nice. (*She moves down* L) If you ask me, she'll eat him up in six months and sling him out.

STELLA. Really, Joan, you don't even know her.

JOAN (*moving* C) I recognize the type.

STELLA. Well, she's very attractive. And terribly smart. One can understand George falling for her.

JOAN. Oh, yes, assisted by a hefty push from her. Puzzles me that she should go to the length of marrying him. I mean, she can't marry them all. One can only assume that George doesn't recognize a hint when he's holding it in his arms.

STELLA. Joan, do stop it.

JOAN. I don't know about you, Stella, but I thought he was cooling off as the wedding approached. I wouldn't blame him, either—after my experience of marriage.

STELLA. Your what?

JOAN. M'm! I certainly let that slip out. (*She moves to* R *of the sofa*)

STELLA. You've been married? (*She rises and moves* RC) Why ever haven't you told us?

JOAN (*sitting on the right arm of the sofa*) It was hardly anything to boast about.

STELLA. What happened?

JOAN. I couldn't stand his absent-mindedness.

STELLA. His absent-mindedness? (*She sits on the left arm of the armchair* C)

JOAN. Whenever another woman came along, he forgot he was married to me. I agree it makes a nice change nowadays that he liked women but one can overdo everything. He liked them in quantities. When his paper gave him the advice column, girls didn't get answers to their problems, they got invitations. I'll have to get round to divorcing him one of these days. (*She rises and moves* L *of the sofa to the window*) Well, well, to think the poor ailing *Gazette* should bring us to a place like this. If it goes on this way, we may even start getting our salaries on time. Still, I suppose it's miracle enough that we manage to struggle into print every week. (*She moves up* c) You know, I can't help wondering whether our two centenarians are going to be comfortable here.

STELLA. Why shouldn't they be?

JOAN (*moving to* L *of Stella*) Would you be—if you'd been small-time farmers and living for the last thirty years in a five-and-six a week cottage in rural England?

STELLA. Our readers wanted it to be done in style. After all, that's why they sent in their sixpences and shillings and pound notes.

JOAN. The suckers! Well, they are. The good old sentimental British Public—always rushing to get up a fund for someone or something—so long, of course, as it isn't anything cultural. Which will be the old couple's bedroom?

STELLA (*rising and indicating the door* L) In there.

JOAN. I'd better take a look. (*She moves to the door* L *and opens it*) Our readers love a touch of glamour. I thought—a shot for our two centenarians being tucked up for the night with a cup of hot cocoa each.

(*The telephone rings.* STELLA *moves to the telephone and lifts the receiver*)

STELLA (*into the telephone*) Penthouse suite . . . Oh, yes . . . (*To Joan*) *News of the World.*

JOAN. Tell them they have the wrong number. This is a *happy* marriage.

(JOAN *exits* L)

STELLA (*into the telephone*) They're called Mr and Mrs Mellowes —(*she sits at the desk*) and they'll have been married eighty years next Saturday. . . . Yes, of course, to each other. . . . Very funny. (*She slams down the receiver*)

(JOAN *enters* L *and moves to* L *of the sofa*)

How do you like that?

JOAN. What?

STELLA. He said that after eighty years of marriage, he'd have thought they'd suffered enough.

JOAN. I say, Stella, have you seen that film star bed in there? It's as big as a tennis court. If we put this frail old couple in that, we'll probably never find them again.

STELLA. Hadn't you better get back to your post before they arrive?

JOAN. What a room! First time I've ever seen pillows that looked erotic. What? (*She moves up* c) Oh, I suppose so. I wonder if that P.R.O. has cooled down yet. Just before I escaped he was telling me my eyes glow with a blend of English purity and Oriental allure. I expect I'll have to clobber him before we leave.

(GEORGE *enters* R *and stands above the armchair* RC)

STELLA. Well?

GEORGE. We're staying.

STELLA. Both of you?

GEORGE. Yes. But only till Mr Elton can find someone else. I had to be rather brutal with her. She's very upset.

JOAN. Well, well, what a masterful type you are.

STELLA. Lay off him, Joan.

JOAN. I mean it. To tame her so soon. This gives me a new respect for you.

(*There is a tap at the double doors.*

PHILLIP SCOTT *enters by the double doors. He is aged about thirty-five, handsome and distinguished-looking. He is elegantly dressed and possesses great charm*)

Now what? (*She moves up* L) Oh, it's you.

SCOTT (*moving up* C) You sound disappointed.

JOAN. Disappointed? First time I ever heard a P.R.O. make an understatement.

SCOTT (*to Stella*) I thought you should know that one or two reporters have turned up to interview the old couple. (*To George*) Incidentally, your coming here with your bride to cover the story makes it a whole lot more interesting.

JOAN. Especially to the bride.

SCOTT. Well, it's a novel angle. The new and the old. One marriage eighty years old and the other fresh this morning.

GEORGE (*moving to* R *of Scott*) Now, see here . . .

JOAN. He's right, George. (*She moves to* L *of Scott*) It has everything. Even suspense interest. Which marriage, the new or the old, will break up first?

GEORGE (*to Scott*) Look, if you so much as breathe a word about my being on honeymoon, there's going to be blood spilt around here.

SCOTT. My dear fellow . . .

GEORGE. I mean it. I've enough trouble on my hands as it is.

(SUSAN *taps and enters by the double doors*)

SUSAN (*to George*) Oh, excuse me, sir, but madam asked me to let you know I've transferred your luggage to bedroom number five.

GEORGE. Oh! Oh, thanks.

SUSAN (*pointing*) At the end of the corridor.

(SUSAN, *repressing a snigger, exits by the double doors*)

JOAN (*crossing below Scott to the double doors*) This must be the quickest trip to the dog-house on record.

GEORGE. You listen to me . . .

Joan. Sorry, duty calls. See you all later.

(Joan *exits by the double doors*)

Scott. I must be off, too. Any problems, Mr Maxwell?
George (*moving to* R *of Scott*) Are you trying to be funny?
Scott. Good Lord, no!
George. If I thought you were . . .
Scott. But I assure you. I mean any problem other than—well, other than . . . (*He crosses quickly to the double doors*) Excuse me. (*To Stella*) Let me know what you want me to do about the reporters.

(Scott *exits by the double doors*)

George. I don't like that fellow.
Stella. So I gathered.
Scott (*off*) Ah, Mr Elton.
Stella. He's here—Mr Elton.
Scott (*off*) Anything you want, just let me know.

(Frederick Elton *enters by the double doors. He is aged about sixty and is stout and florid, and tends to irascibility. He is wearing his hat and a light top coat and carries a brief-case.* Stella *rises*)

Elton (*as he enters; over his shoulder*) I'll want you shortly.
Scott (*off*) Any time, Mr Elton. At your service.

(Elton *closes the doors and moves to* R *of George.* Stella *moves to* R *of Elton*)

Elton. Well, Maxwell, I trust you've settled everything satisfactorily. (*He puts his brief-case on the bar*)

(Stella *relieves Elton of his hat and coat and puts them on the window-seat*)

George (*moving up* L) I've settled I want to be taken off this story.
Elton (*moving to* R *of the sofa*) Well, you can't be.
George. Look, sir . . .
Elton. You're a newspaperman first and a bridegroom afterwards.
George. Why can't Peters handle it? Just because those superannuated nuts insisted on me . . .

(Stella *collects Elton's brief-case, crosses and puts it on the desk, then sits on the desk chair*)

Elton. They didn't.
George. But your message said . . .
Elton. I had to give some reason. (*He sits on the sofa, at the right end of it*) I certainly couldn't give the truth. My God, when I think how near I got to becoming the laughing-stock of Fleet Street.

GEORGE (*moving to* L *of the sofa*) I don't follow.

ELTON. Then I'll tell you. Here we are, honouring two people whose example is an inspiration to all who cherish the institution of marriage. And that includes Miss Jessop but for whom this story would occupy a column and then get lost. And who do I put in charge of them? Why the hell didn't someone tell me Peters had deserted his wife to live with a barmaid from the *Black Lion?*

GEORGE. Peters has!

ELTON. I only found out by the merest chance.

GEORGE. Who'd have believed it! Still, why not . . . ?

ELTON. Why not someone else from what we laughably call our newsroom? I'll tell you why. Because Peters isn't the worst of them, only the oldest. Those who aren't carrying on with other men's wives have littered the town with their misbegotten brats. We don't have a newsroom; we have a moral cesspool.

GEORGE. Well, I know that one or two of them . . .

ELTON. And to think the *Gazette* is owned by a maiden lady who devotes her life to succouring unmarried mothers. I should say that most of them are put in the family way by her own staff. If she found out, she'd proably sack the lot of us—including me. Do you think I'd get another job on a paper at my age?

GEORGE. No, sir, of course you wouldn't.

ELTON (*rising*) Damn it, there's no need to agree with me so heartily.

GEORGE. Sorry, sir.

ELTON (*moving* RC) So I'm left with you. God help me! Even you can't have formed an adulterous relationship within four hours of getting married—though I could be wrong even about that.

(*The telephone rings.* STELLA *lifts the receiver*)

STELLA (*into the telephone*) Penthouse suite . . . Hold on . . . (*To Elton*) It's Mr Scott, the P.R.O. here. Asking if he should bring the reporters up.

ELTON. What reporters?

STELLA. A few have turned up to interview Mr and Mrs Mellowes.

ELTON. I should have thought they'd have had something better to do. Tell him to ask them to wait.

STELLA (*into the telephone*) Mr Elton says they're to wait . . . Hold on . . . (*To Elton*) The man from the *Courier* is amongst them.

ELTON. Tell him to go to hell. (*He moves up* C) The *Gazette* will cover East Anglia.

STELLA (*into the telephone*) No *Courier* man . . . Right. (*She replaces the receiver*)

GEORGE (*moving to* L *of Elton*) Then it's out of the question to take me off the story?

ELTON. Quite out of the question. Where is your wife?

GEORGE (*indicating the door* R) In there. She's very upset.

ELTON. I dare say she is, but she's got to find out sooner or later what it's like being married to a newspaper-man.

STELLA. I was wondering, Mr Elton—perhaps Joan and I could manage.

ELTON. Nonsense! Your job is to see that the schedule is kept to. That'll take all your time. It's a heavy programme and a number of important people are involved. I want nothing to go wrong with that. Anyway, what's all the fuss about? It's only for three days. (*He crosses down* L) When I was married I had no honeymoon at all. If you like to fetch her out, I'll talk to her.

GEORGE (*crossing towards the door* R) No, thanks.

ELTON. Suit yourself. What the devil's keeping the old people? They should have been here by now.

STELLA (*rising and moving* C) When will you have the reporters up?

ELTON. After we've seen the old couple and got our own story.

STELLA (*moving to the bar*) Shall I see to the drinks?

ELTON. Yes. Where are they? Oh, over there. Mind you don't hand them out too fast. Oh, and put the bottles of beer conspicuously in the front. No need to go out of our way to encourage them to guzzle whisky and gin. (*He sits on the sofa, at the left end of it*)

(STELLA *rearranges the bottles*)

Where's Joan?

STELLA. Waiting for them downstairs.

ELTON. You sure she knows what I want?

STELLA. Quite sure.

ELTON. Where's my speech of welcome?

STELLA. I have it ready.

ELTON. We'll print that in full.

GEORGE. Yes, sir, of course.

ELTON. By the way, they won't know me so you'd better tell them who I am. Then I'll formally welcome them and put them at their ease. I dare say at first they'll be overwhelmed by it all, seeing what age they are. Then I'll turn them over to you to get the first instalment of the story. That clear?

GEORGE. Perfectly.

ELTON. It had better be. Miss Jessop is following every word of this story and I'm not having anything go wrong with it.

STELLA (*moving to the desk chair and sitting*) I don't think you need worry.

ELTON. I'm already worrying. By the time this is over there'll be three centenarians here, not two.

(JOAN *enters by the double doors*)

JOAN. They're here. Coming now. (*She stands above the doorway*) This way, please.

(ELTON *rises and crosses above the sofa to* L *of Joan.* STELLA *rises.*
GEORGE *stands* R *of the double doors.*

HENRY MELLOWES *and* SARAH MELLOWES, *his wife, appear in
the open doorway.* HENRY *has white bushy eyebrows and a straggling
white moustache. He wears a suit of bygone cut with a heavy watch chain
across his middle. He leans on a stick. Although he tends to drop off now
and again, he is merry and alert.* SARAH *is taller than Henry and carries
herself well without the aid of a stick, but she wears spectacles. Her clothes,
too, are of an earlier period.*

ELIZABETH WELLING, *the* NURSE *and* SCOTT *follow Henry and
Sarah on. The* NURSE *is middle-aged, stout and fussy.* JOAN *moves
quickly* RC, *turns and takes a flash photograph of the group in the open
doorway*)

ELTON. Come in, Mr Mellowes—Mrs Mellowes. It's a great
pleasure to meet you. Welcome to the penthouse suite of the *Royal
Park Hotel.*

(HENRY *comes into the room and stands up* C. SARAH *follows to* R *of
Henry. The* NURSE *and* SCOTT *stand in the doorway*)

HENRY. The what suite?
ELTON (*crossing to* L *of Henry*) Penthouse suite. Perhaps in the
circumstances I might say the bridal suite.
HENRY. Well, there's no harm in saying it.
ELTON. By the way, I'm Mr Elton, the editor—seeing I have to
introduce myself.
HENRY. My name's Mellowes—Henry Mellowes.
ELTON. I know.
HENRY. And this here's Sarah, my wife.
ELTON. Yes, I do know.
HENRY. Oh, who told you?
ELTON. I—er . . . Do come and sit down, both of you. (*He indicates
the sofa*) Mrs Mellowes.
SARAH (*moving below the sofa*) Thank you, sir. Thank you kindly.
ELTON. I must say you don't look anything like your great age.
You're even able to walk without assistance.
SARAH. I should be. I've been doing it since I was nine months
old. (*She sits on the sofa at the left end of it*)

(JOAN *smothers a laugh*)

ELTON. Yes, quite, quite. Mr Mellowes, here beside your wife.
HENRY (*moving below the sofa*) Right you are.
ELTON (*moving to* R *of Henry*) I won't introduce you to everyone.
You know Mr Maxwell, of course.
HENRY. Ah, yes, good afternoon, young fellow. You got any
more of them stories you told me last time? Proper scorchers, they
was. Particularly that one about . . .
GEORGE. Mr Mellowes, do sit down.

HENRY. What? Oh, yes. Just a minute. (*Supported by his stick, he laboriously deposits his rear on the sofa, at the right end of it*) Ah! That's it.

(ELTON *moves above the sofa*)

NURSE (*moving* C) Mr Elton, there's something . . .
ELTON. One moment, Nurse.
NURSE. But I think . . .
ELTON. In a moment. Stella!

(STELLA *takes a copy of Elton's speech from his brief-case, a note-pad and pencil from her own case, crosses to Elton, gives him the copy of the speech, then crosses to the window up* L)

Thanks. (*He moves down* L *and turns*)

(JOAN *joins Stella. The* NURSE *stands with* SCOTT *up* RC)

Mr and Mrs Mellowes . . .
HENRY. That's right. I'm Mr and she's Mrs.
ELTON. Thank you for enlightening me. I should like to say a few words . . .

(HENRY *beckons to* GEORGE *who crosses to him*)

HENRY (*in a loud whisper*) Who did he say he was?
GEORGE. Mr Elton—our editor.
HENRY. Oh, ah! I forget things, you know. I'm getting on, you see.
GEORGE. I know.
HENRY. Nearly a hundred. And I don't always remember things.
GEORGE. Quite.
HENRY. That's on account of me memory not being what it were.
GEORGE. Yes, I'm sure we quite understand. (*To Elton*) Carry on, sir.
ELTON. Thank you very much. On behalf of the *County Gazette* . . .
HENRY. On behalf of the what?
ELTON. The *County Gazette*.
HENRY. Oh! You'll have to speak up a bit. Me hearing isn't what it used to be.
ELTON. Very well.
HENRY. I'm getting on, you see. Nearly a hundred, I am.
ELTON. You told us.
HENRY. Told you what?
ELTON. That you're nearly a hundred.
HENRY. Well, I am.
ELTON. I know you are. I didn't say you were not.
HENRY. Who says I'm not?
ELTON. No-one. May I continue?
HENRY. May you what?
ELTON. Continue with my speech.

HENRY. Oh, you're making a speech, are you?

ELTON. I'm trying.

HENRY. Well, why don't you get on with it?

ELTON. Thank you, I will. On behalf of the *County Gazette*, it gives me great pleasure in welcoming you, Mr Mellowes, and your wife, to the *Royal Park Hotel*. To be not only a hundred years old but to have been married for eighty years is an achievement almost without parallel and, as far as we can trace, the first in our county.

(HENRY, *having dropped off, snores*)

You can imagine with what excitement . . .

(HENRY *snores*)

GEORGE. Oh, Lord, I remember! This is the old man's weakness, sir.

(HENRY *snores*)

ELTON. Well, stop him making that foul noise, can't you?

GEORGE. Yes, sir. (*He shakes Henry*) Mr Mellowes! Mr Mellowes, wake up.

SARAH. I might have knowd he'd make a spectacle of hisself.

HENRY (*waking*) M'm! What? Oh, we got there, then. (*He struggles to rise*)

GEORGE. No, no, this is the hotel. You're already here.

ELTON. For Heaven's sake!

HENRY. The hotel, eh? Bless me, so it is. I was having such a dream. There was this girl . . .

ELTON. Later, Mr Mellowes. Later.

HENRY. What you say?

ELTON. You can tell us about your dream later.

HENRY. What dream?

ELTON. The dream . . . Oh, never mind. (*He crumples the speech and flings it away*) Let's forget it. Maxwell, I'm handing them over to you.

GEORGE. Right you are, sir. (*He moves* RC)

NURSE (*moving up* C; *to Elton*) May I speak now?

ELTON. My good woman, do please stop interrupting. We have work to do. There's a whole lot of reporters waiting downstairs. All right, Maxwell, get on with it.

GEORGE. Yes, sir. (*He sits in the armchair* C) Mrs Mellowes—Mr Mellowes—you know what we have arranged for your three days here. We hope you'll enjoy it. You're visiting the Houses of Parliament, St Paul's, the Abbey and other places of historic interest. On Saturday, as the climax, there'll be a big dinner here. You'll be the guests of honour and all your many relations will be present. The Queen is sending a message of congratulation. And the *County Gazette* has bought the cottage in which you are passing, happily together, your declining years and will present it to you.

(HENRY *is seen to be dozing off again*)

Stella, keep him awake, will you?

(STELLA *moves, perches on the right arm of the sofa and gently shakes* HENRY *into wakefulness*)

HENRY. Why, hello, my dear, where did you spring from? Like a ray of purest sunshine you are.
STELLA. Thank you.
ELTON. Well, thank God we've found out what keeps him alert.

(JOAN *moves quickly down* c, *turns and takes a flash photograph of Stella and Henry, then joins Elton down* L)

JOAN. The thing that keeps all men alert.

(STELLA *rises and moves above the sofa*)

GEORGE. Yes, well, to proceed. Our readers want to hear all about the things you do while you're here and I am going to write it. Other newspapers are interested, too. Some reporters are waiting downstairs to ask you some questions.
SARAH. What about?
GEORGE. About your marriage which, you must realize, is an inspiration to all who are embarking on the path of matrimony.
JOAN. Present company excepted, of course.

(GEORGE *represses a comment.* STELLA *prepares to take notes*)

GEORGE. Mrs Mellowes, tell me, in order that we may pass it on to the others, what would you say is the secret of your highly successful marriage?
SARAH. Well, now, I don't rightly know.
GEORGE. Give and take, perhaps?
SARAH. Aye, that's it. Give and take and making sure from the start I got me own way about everything.
GEORGE. I wonder if Mr Mellowes would agree with that. Never mind. Mr Mellowes, what does it feel like to be a hundred?
HENRY. What do it feel like? Bloody horrible!
GEORGE. Oh, come, Mr Mellowes, you don't mean that.
HENRY. Oh, don't I! How would you like it not being allowed to eat anything you fancy and mustn't have no baccy in your pipe, and your legs won't do what you tell 'em, and when it comes to women you can't hardly remember . . .
GEORGE. Yes, quite, Mr Mellowes, we get your point.
HENRY. 'Tisn't living. Not proper living. Now, you take . . .
GEORGE. We quite understand, Mr Mellowes.
HENRY. I ain't finished yet.
GEORGE (*rising and moving* c) Yes, you have.
ELTON. Now, just a minute . . .

GEORGE. Don't worry, sir. It'll be all right. Tell me, Mr Mellowes, what is your opinion of present-day youth?

HENRY. Youth?

GEORGE. The young people of today. The boys and girls.

HENRY. Well, they're very pretty. Very pretty and feminine.

GEORGE. What about the boys?

HENRY. I was talking about the boys.

(JOAN *moves and stands* L *of Stella above the sofa*)

ELTON. What *is* this?

GEORGE. It's wonderful how he's retained his sense of humour, isn't it, sir? What about the girls, Mr Mellowes? How do they differ from the girls of your young days?

HENRY. Well, a bit slimmer perhaps.

GEORGE. I mean in their ways. For instance, would you say their morals were stricter when you were a young man?

SARAH. Not when he was around they weren't.

ELTON. What the devil does this mean? (*He moves to* L *of the sofa*) Maxwell, you didn't tell me . . .

GEORGE. She was only joking, weren't you, Mrs Mellowes?

SARAH. I was not. If I was to tell you . . .

GEORGE. Isn't it wonderful, sir, the way they're pulling our legs at their age?

ELTON. Pulling our legs?

GEORGE. Well, of course, sir. I think it's absolutely marvellous. I might concentrate on it, don't you think, sir? Well, we mustn't keep those news-hounds waiting. Mrs Mellowes, one thing you're sure to be asked. In all your eighty years of marriage, what stands out most vividly in your memory?

SARAH. Let me see . . .

GEORGE. Your wedding day? Your first christening?

SARAH. No.

GEORGE. Then what?

SARAH. The first time he hit me.

GEORGE. Oh, Lord! (*He moves to the desk and sits at it*)

SARAH. It weren't the last time, neither. I can remember . . .

ELTON. Oh, no, you can't. (*He crosses to* C) Maxwell, you damn fool, why didn't you tell me they were like this?

GEORGE. I didn't know.

ELTON. Then you should have known.

GEORGE. The daughter they live with gave me a string of lies.

ELTON. (*brushing past George*) Mr Scott, go down and get rid of those reporters.

SCOTT. Well, I suppose I'd better.

ELTON. Say our guests are too tired after their journey to see anyone and we'll give them a story.

SCOTT. Right.

GEORGE (*rising*) If you'd like me to go with Mr Scott . . .

ELTON. No——

(GEORGE *resumes his seat*)

—you and I are going to have a little talk. What the blazes do you mean by it?

(SCOTT *exits by the double doors*)

NURSE (*moving to* L *of Elton*) Perhaps you'd like to hear what I have to say now.

ELTON. Must you keep bothering me, Nurse?

NURSE. Very well. I intend to leave, anyway.

ELTON. Leave? What for?

NURSE. They're impossible, quite impossible. I had nothing but insults the whole way here in the car. I mean, one expects a little trouble with old people but I've never in all my experience had to contend with anything like this. Mrs Mellowes is the worst. (*She moves to* R *of the sofa*)

SARAH (*rising*) Oh, I am, am I?

ELTON. Now, wait a minute . . .

NURSE. Your behaviour has been quite inexcusable.

GEORGE. Nurse, please, take it easy.

NURSE. That's all very well for you. You don't know the things she said to me.

SARAH. And I meant 'em.

(*The* NURSE *moves to* L *of Elton*)

ELTON. Oh, my God!

SARAH. I'm not having no fusspot of a nurse following me around like I was a sick child. I never have and I'm not going to start now.

HENRY. She's off!

ELTON (*crossing to* R *of the sofa*) Now, listen, Mrs Mellowes, I engaged Nurse Welling . . .

SARAH. Well, you can unengage her because I'm not having her.

ELTON. That's for me to decide.

SARAH. Oh, is it? Well, if she don't go, I go.

ELTON. What! Now, see here . . .

STELLA (*moving down* L *of the sofa*) I do see her point, Mr Elton. I know I'd feel the same if I were as fit as Mrs Mellowes at her age.

ELTON. I don't care how fit . . .

STELLA. After all, who wants to be watched over by a uniformed nurse when you're perfectly well?

SARAH. Quite right, my girl. You got a lot of sense. You're pretty, too.

STELLA. Not so pretty as you were, I'm sure.

SARAH. I wasn't bad and that's the truth.

STELLA. So why don't we let nurse stay, just in case any of us needs her, but she mustn't wear her uniform?

SARAH. I don't know about that.

STELLA. We'll soon forget she's a nurse without her uniform. To please me. We are responsible, you know.

SARAH. Well, when you put it like that . . .

(STELLA *seats* SARAH *back on the sofa*)

ELTON (*moving up* c) Well, thank God we can agree on something.

NURSE. You may but I'm still leaving.

ELTON. You'll do as you're told. Haven't we got enough trouble as it is?

NURSE. You don't know the half of it yet.

ELTON. What are you talking about?

NURSE. I've been trying to tell you for the past twenty minutes.

ELTON. Tell me what? (*He moves to* L *of the Nurse*) Do you want to drive me mad?

NURSE. I've had a lot to do with old people. I know their cranky ways. I've learned how to deal with their obstinacy and their silliness . . .

ELTON. Damn it, woman, come to the point.

NURSE. Very well. This wonderful sweet old couple of yours, this loving husband and devoted wife you're parading before the world, are going to make you look very foolish. I dread to think what your readers are going to say when they find out.

ELTON. Find out what, for Pete's sake?

NURSE. Only that six months ago they had such a violent quarrel the last of many I might add, that they haven't spoken a word to each other since.

ELTON. No! I don't believe it.

NURSE. What's more, with the cussedness of the very old, they swear they won't ever speak to one another again.

ELTON. They can't do this to me. I won't have it.

NURSE. Well, you needn't think you can patch up their quarrel, because you can't. No-one can.

ELTON. Why not?

NURSE. Because they've now forgotten what it was they quarrelled about. Ask them.

ELTON (*moving to* R *of the sofa; to Henry*) Is this true?

HENRY. She ain't speaking to me, if that's what you mean.

ELTON (*to Sarah*) Why not? How the devil can you behave so childishly at your age?

SARAH. I don't know what business it is of yours, but since you ask, I'll tell you. We been together too long. We get on each other's nerves. We got nothing to do the live-long day but sit either side of our fireplace, looking at one another.

HENRY. Aye, that's the truth of it.

SARAH. I never did like him all that much. Now I can't abide him—haven't been able to for the past forty year or more.

ELTON (*crossing to George*) My God, I'll never be able to live this down. Maxwell, you idiot!

GEORGE (*rising*) How was I to know?

ELTON. You wrote the story, didn't you? This'll finish me. (*He moves up* C) My God, Miss Jessop!

NURSE. Well, now you know I'll say good day to you. (*She moves to the double doors*)

ELTON. No—wait. Come back.

NURSE. No, thank you.

ELTON. You can't go off like this.

NURSE. Oh, yes, I can.

(*The* NURSE *exits by the double doors*)

ELTON. Stella, go after her. We can't have her blabbing this all over the place.

(STELLA *crosses and exits by the double doors. The telephone rings*)

Now what? (*To George*) Answer that.

(GEORGE *sits on the desk chair and lifts the telephone receiver*)

GEORGE (*into the telephone*) Penthouse suite . . .

SARAH. Now, see here, I don't know what's going on . . .

ELTON (*moving down* C) Be quiet.

GEORGE (*into the telephone*) Just a minute . . .

HENRY (*to Elton*) Don't you talk to my Sarah like that.

(HENRY *and* SARAH *struggle to their feet*)

GEORGE (*to Elton*) The P.R.O. is having a little difficulty with those reporters.

ELTON. Blast! Say you'll be down in a minute.

GEORGE (*into the telephone*) I'll be down. (*He replaces the receiver*)

HENRY. Now then, Mr Whatever-you're-called . . .

ELTON. Oh, for heaven's sake, get them both out of my sight. (*He moves up* R)

JOAN. Yes, come along, you two.

SARAH. Where we going?

JOAN. To your room. (*She moves to the door* L *and opens it*) You both need a rest after all this excitement. And if you don't, we certainly do. Come along. You, too, Mr Mellowes.

HENRY. We didn't ask to be brought here, you know. Maybe we should go back home.

JOAN. Nonsense! (*She moves to* L *of Sarah*) The fun's only just started, hasn't it, Mr Elton?

ELTON. Do you mind not trying to be funny.

JOAN (*indicating the door* L) This way.

SARAH (*crossing below Joan to the door* L) Here, we only got one room between us?

JOAN. Yes, but what a room. Take a look at it.

SARAH. I'm used to a room of me own. He snores like an old pig.

HENRY (*crossing to Sarah*) That's a lie. I never snored in me life.

SARAH. What were you doing just now? Tell me what that was if it wasn't snoring.

(HENRY *and* SARAH, *still arguing, exit* L)

JOAN. Well, at least I've got them to speak to one another again.

(JOAN *exits* L, *closing the door behind her*)

GEORGE (*rising*) I'll be nipping downstairs, then.

ELTON (*moving down* C) Not yet you won't. What do you mean by it?

GEORGE (*moving* RC) It could have happened to anyone, sir.

ELTON. But it doesn't. Only to you. (*He moves to* L *of George*) Since I made the unpardonable mistake of adding you to the staff, I've printed more apologies than news.

GEORGE. One apology, sir.

ELTON. Don't interrupt me. (*He crosses below the sofa to* L *of it*) How could you have done it? That's what I ask myself. You must have realized what they were like.

GEORGE. But you see, sir . . .

ELTON. Don't interrupt. (*He crosses above the sofa to* C) I've got to think. You know what the British public is like. Nothing touches their hearts so much as stories about dumb animals, babies and old people—in that order. And what are we serving up to our readers? A couple of senile fighting cocks.

GEORGE (*moving down* R) It's possible our readers might be amused.

ELTON (*moving down* C) Amused! Amused!

GEORGE. Well, at least it's different.

ELTON. Are you out of your mind?

GEORGE. I only thought . . .

ELTON. Do you dare to stand there and suggest that, having presented those two as the Darby and Joan of all time, having got our readers to get up a fund to bring them here, we now reveal them to be two cynical centenarians sharing only one thought—that they can't bear the sight of each other? In this country that would practically amount to sacrilege.

GEORGE. I do see your point, sir.

ELTON. I'm relieved to hear it. (*He sits on the right arm of the sofa*) No, there's only one thing to do. We go on as we began. They're devoted to one another, you understand? They can scarcely bear to be out of sight of each other. They pass their few remaining years, sitting side by side, hand in hand, looking back at the years they have spent happily together.

GEORGE (*moving* RC) Look, sir . . .

ELTON. Shut up! Their love for each other is as fresh and tender as on that far-off day when, she a shy wispy girl and he a young man with the down still fair on his upper lip, fate brought them together and there began a love that will endure into eternity. Oh, and you might mention that when their tired old eyes meet, they light up with a glow that is strangely ethereal—that sort of thing. You understand?

GEORGE. Only too well, sir.

ELTON. And cut the sarcasm, if you don't mind. If we want to be believed, we've got to lay it on thick.

GEORGE. Yes, sir.

ELTON (*rising*) And you see those two crackpots behave themselves in public. They're going to be a happily married couple if it kills them.

GEORGE (*moving to* R *of Elton*) Leave it to me, sir.

ELTON (*moving down* L) Now get downstairs and pacify those reporters.

GEORGE. Right. (*He moves to the double doors*)

ELTON. If the *Courier* gets hold of this, we're sunk.

GEORGE. Why should they?

ELTON. Because they're smart, because they've got some good men—which is a damn sight more than I have. (*He moves up* C) Perhaps I'd better come with you.

GEORGE. I don't think . . .

ELTON. Well, I do.

(GEORGE *opens the door for Elton*)

After the mess you've made of things, I daren't trust you.

(ELTON *exits by the double doors.* GEORGE *is about to follow.*
BRENDA *enters* R)

BRENDA. George, I want to talk to you.

GEORGE. Later. You'll never guess what's happened now.

BRENDA (*crossing to* R *of the sofa*) I don't have to. I heard it all. And for this you've ruined our honeymoon.

ELTON (*off; calling*) Maxwell!

GEORGE. Sorry, I've got to go.

(GEORGE *exits by the double doors*)

BRENDA. George! (*She stamps her foot in rage*)

(*The telephone rings*)

(*She crosses to the telephone and angrily lifts the receiver. Into the telephone*)
Yes? . . . No, he isn't here . . . I don't know when he will be back . . . Who? . . . The *Courier?* . . . (*A smile spreads over her face*) Perhaps I can tell you what you want to know. Have you a pencil and paper ready? . . . (*She sits at the desk*) I'll wait with pleasure . . .

CURTAIN

ACT II

SCENE—*The same. The following morning.*

When the CURTAIN *rises,* JOAN *is sitting on the sofa, fitting a new film into her camera. The flowers have been removed from the pedestals. There is a knock at the double doors.* SCOTT *enters by the double doors and moves* C.

SCOTT. Good morning.

JOAN. 'Morning.

SCOTT. Everything under control?

JOAN. Yes. Especially me. You know, I don't think I thanked you properly last night for coming to my room to see I had everything I wanted.

SCOTT. One does one's best.

JOAN. How's you foot feeling? So stupid of me to slam the door on it like that.

SCOTT (*moving to* R *of the sofa*) In my profession one expects setbacks—temporary ones, of course.

JOAN. Perhaps you should let Nurse take a look at it.

SCOTT. I hardly recognized her out of uniform. Who talked her into staying?

JOAN. Stella, of course. She even got those two senile delinquents to talk to one another.

SCOTT. And where are they?

JOAN (*indicating the door* L) In there, husbanding their strength for today's programme—I hope.

SCOTT (*sitting on the right arm of the sofa*) Which reminds me. Perhaps you could tell Miss Haley: everything's fixed for Sir Rupert Hoxon to give them lunch at the House of Commons.

JOAN. Sir Rupert will never be the same again.

SCOTT. Also their interview for Radio Newsreel is on this morning. a fellow called "Wallcott-Brown" is coming.

JOAN. Let's hope those two comics give him the answers George has written out for them. I don't think our beloved editor would survive another incident like yesterday's.

SCOTT. Nor would the *Gazette*. You might find yourself looking for a job.

JOAN. It's happened before. Anyway, I've decided to leave the *Gazette*.

SCOTT (*rising*) Why is that?

JOAN. I find my duties force me to associate with so many undesirable characters.

SCOTT. You interest me. (*He sits* R *of Joan on the sofa*) I keep asking myself what causes all this cynicism and sardonic humour. Could it be a horror of showing any warmth of feeling?

JOAN. Not at all. (*She rises*) I wouldn't reveal this to anyone, but the fact is I've never been the same since I discovered I had the gift of reading people's thoughts—especially men's. (*She moves down* L)

SCOTT (*rising, moving up* C *and looking at the pedestals*) No flowers! That's odd. The florist usually does this suite first. I'll have to remind her.

JOAN (*putting her camera on the table* L) Go right ahead.

SCOTT. If you're serious about leaving the *Gazette* I might be able to help. (*He moves to* R *of the sofa*)

JOAN. Thanks, but it's quite easy to leave. All I have to do . . .

SCOTT. I mean I might be able to offer you a job. I'm leaving here to start my own public relations business.

JOAN (*moving down* L *of the sofa*) Congratulations!

SCOTT (*moving above the sofa*) I'll need a right-hand man—or woman.

JOAN. Well, I dare say there are plenty of right-handed women about.

SCOTT. You wouldn't know anyone that would fit the bill? Someone of your own calibre—nice to look at, elegant, self-assured, lots of experience of the world and of people.

JOAN (*crossing below the sofa to* RC) Now, who do I know who is nice-looking, elegant, self-assured, experienced—and half-witted?

SCOTT (*moving to* L *of Joan*) You've got me all wrong. Why not let me tell you more about it? Say, tonight. There's a little restaurant I'd like you to try.

JOAN. I've tried it. The service was terrible. And there was a man with a red beard who kept throwing his spaghetti at the head waiter.

SCOTT (*taking her hand*) My dear girl . . .

JOAN (*releasing herself*) Look, so I don't have to spend the rest of the week wrestling with you, let's get something straight. (*She crosses below Scott to* C) You're wasting your valuable time on me. I've been around too long. It would take more than a wolf in P.R.O. clothing to bowl me over. If all the men who had unsuccessfully invited me to give my all were lined up, the last of them would need to have a very great deal of patience indeed. Apart from which, I have enjoyed for a brief while what is humorously described as married bliss. As a result I'm immunized against men, a state of mind I confidently recommend to all right-thinking women. Is that clear? (*She moves below the sofa*)

SCOTT (*moving to* R *of Joan*) It's clear that some fool of a man has hurt you badly. I shall do my best to make it up to you.

JOAN. Now, look . . .

SCOTT. No, no don't thank me yet. There's heaps of time.

(GEORGE *enters* R, *looking disconsolate*)

JOAN. Why, George, what are you doing in your wife's bedroom? (*She moves down* L) I mean—oh, you know what I mean.
GEORGE. Have you seen her this morning?
JOAN. No. You don't mean she's gone?
GEORGE. No. Her things are still in there.
SCOTT (*moving to the double doors*) I have to go and find the florist. If I see your wife, I'll tell her.
GEORGE. Thanks.

(SCOTT *exits by the double doors*)

JOAN. Cheer up, George. Everything will come right after Saturday, you'll see.
GEORGE (*moving to the bar*) I'm not waiting till Saturday. I'm clearing out now.
JOAN. This morning?
GEORGE. Yes.
JOAN. Mr Elton will not be pleased. (*She collects her camera*)
GEORGE. I can't help that. I should never have let him bully me into staying. It wasn't fair to Brenda. Anyway, she's leaving this morning with or without me.

(BRENDA *enters by the double doors*)

Brenda! (*He moves to Brenda to embrace her*)
BRENDA (*evading George and moving down* R) I gather you want to see me.

(JOAN *crosses to the double doors with her camera dangling from her hand by its strap*)

JOAN. You will excuse me. I have to take my camera for its morning walk. I expect I'll see you both before you go.

(JOAN *exits by the double doors*)

BRENDA. What did she mean—before we go?
GEORGE (*moving up* C) We're clearing out of here.
BRENDA. We?
GEORGE. Yes. I've had enough.
BRENDA. I see.
GEORGE (*moing down* C) Aren't you pleased?
BRENDA. I'd have been more pleased if you'd made this decision yesterday and spared me all this humiliation.
GEORGE (*moving to her*) Brenda, do you mind! (*He attempts to embrace her*)

(BRENDA *evades George's embrace by crossing below him to* C)

BRENDA. At least I'd have known I came first with you.
GEORGE (*moving to* R *of her*) But you do.

BRENDA (*moving below the sofa*) You've made us both look utterly ridiculous.

GEORGE (*following her*) Have a heart! I've admitted I was wrong but it was a damn difficult situation.

BRENDA. Very well—so long as we go. Have you packed?

GEORGE. Not yet. I'll do it right away.

BRENDA. Please do. I'll believe all this when we're actually off the premises.

(*There is a knock at the double doors.*
SCOTT *enters by the double doors, carrying two vases of arranged flowers*)

SCOTT. I'm sorry. Is it all right if I . . . ?

GEORGE. What? Oh, yes, go ahead.

(SCOTT *places both vases on the bar*)

(*To Brenda*) I'll be packed in ten minutes.

(GEORGE *exits* R. SCOTT *picks up one vase and puts it on the pedestal up* R)

SCOTT. So you're leaving us, Mrs Maxwell? Can't say I blame you. If you'll forgive me for saying so, though, it won't solve your problem.

BRENDA (*sitting on the sofa*) What do you mean?

SCOTT (*moving up* c) No. I'm afraid I'm intruding.

BRENDA. Let's pretend you're not.

SCOTT (*picking up the second vase*) It's just that you've married a newspaperman. This is what your life is going to be like.

BRENDA. Then he won't be a newspaperman for long.

SCOTT (*putting the vase on the pedestal up* L) Ah, but you won't get him to give it up that easily—unless . . .

BRENDA. Unless what?

SCOTT. There might be one way. I'm leaving here. It's just possible I could make you a business proposition that would solve your difficulties.

BRENDA. And your difficulties, too, presumably?

SCOTT (*moving to* L *of the sofa*) I don't deny it.

BRENDA. How much would it cost me?

SCOTT. Very little. (*He bends over the left arm of the sofa towards Brenda*) This is hardly the time to explain it all. Perhaps I could ring you?

BRENDA (*rising and moving* c) I'll think about it.

SCOTT. It will cost you nothing to listen.

BRENDA (*moving to the door* R) I've said I'll think about it.

(BRENDA *exits* R. SCOTT *gazes after her with a satisfied smile.*
SUSAN *enters by the double doors and moves up* c)

SCOTT (*moving to* L *of Susan*) What do you want?

SUSAN. Philip . . .
SCOTT. Don't call me that.
SUSAN. I'm sorry but I've got to talk to you.
SCOTT. Not here.
SUSAN. But there's never any chance . . .
SCOTT. Not here, I said. I'll see you downstairs.
SUSAN. But you've said that before. Philip, please . . .

(STELLA *enters by the double doors and moves* RC)

Will that be all, Mr Scott?
SCOTT. Yes, that's all.

(SUSAN *exits by the double doors*)

Ah, Miss Haley. And looking so preoccupied.
STELLA. It's time to get the old people ready for the day's pro-
gramme. Have you seen Miss Banstead?
SCOTT. She was here just now. I'll see if I can find her for you.

(SCOTT *exits by the double doors. The telephone rings.* STELLA *moves
to the telephone and lifts the receiver*)

STELLA (*into the telephone*) Penthouse suite . . . No, but I can give
him a message . . . Oh, Mr Wallcott-Brown . . . That'll be half an
hour earlier than we said . . . I think so . . . Right, I'll tell him. (*She
depresses the receiver*) Nurse Welling's room, please . . .

(JOAN *enters by the double doors and puts her camera on the table* RC)

JOAN (*moving to Stella*) Looking for me, Stella?
STELLA. It's time the old people turned out. (*Into the telephone*) Oh,
Nurse, could you come now, please? . . . Thanks. (*She replaces the
receiver*)

(HENRY *enters* L, *wearing a dressing-gown over his pyjamas*)

HENRY. Where is it? (*He crosses to* C) Come on now, where is it?
STELLA. Where is what?
HENRY. My suit. Someone's gone and pinched my suit.
STELLA. No, no.
HENRY. They has, I tell you. I left it folded over a chair like I
always does and now it's gone.
STELLA. The valet has it.
HENRY. What's that?
STELLA. The valet has it.
HENRY. Has he! Well, he ain't getting away with it. I paid four
pound for that there suit—back in nineteen-~~thirty~~-four and I'm
not letting no dirty thief take it off of me.   forty
STELLA. But he's only pressing it.
HENRY. What's that?
STELLA. We want you to look smart. (*She crosses to* R *of Henry*)
He's pressing it for you.

HENRY. He's got no right. It don't want no pressing. It's took me all these years to get it to my shape.

STELLA. Mr Mellowes . . .

HENRY. You get my suit back this instant, do you hear?

JOAN. All right. Calm down, you little firebrand. (*She lifts the telephone receiver*)

HENRY. And don't you call me no names, neither.

JOAN (*into the telephone*) Valet service, please . . .

HENRY. Far too many women around here. Bossy lot you all are, too.

JOAN. I can see we're going to have trouble with you.

STELLA. Of course we're not, are we, Mr Mellowes?

JOAN (*into the telephone*) Oh, send Mr Mellowes' suit along, will you? . . . Thanks. (*She replaces the receiver*)

HENRY. Damned impudence taking my clothes. Them trousers was just right for sitting down in.

STELLA. We're very sorry and we won't do it again.

HENRY. I should hope not. (*He moves to the door* L) Can't put a thing down in this place without someone whips it away. It's come to something when a man ain't got no control of his own trousers. 'Tain't dignified not having your own trousers. So you leave 'em alone, do you hear?

STELLA (*moving to him*) Yes, Mr Mellowes.

HENRY (*muttering*) Women! Interfering lot of busybodies. Never let you alone, they won't.

(HENRY *exits* L)

JOAN (*moving to the bar*) For our Henry that was quite an animated conversation.

(STELLA *moves to Joan up* C. *There is a knock at the double doors.* SUSAN *enters by the double doors, carrying Henry's suit*)

STELLA (*indicating the door* L) In there, please.

SUSAN (*crossing to the door* L) We had rather a job with this but we've done our best.

(SUSAN *taps on the door* L *and exits*)

JOAN. She's very pretty, that girl. What's her name?

STELLA. "Susan", I think.

(SUSAN *off* L, *is heard to shriek, then she enters hurriedly* L *and moves above the sofa*)

What's happened?

SUSAN. Did you say that old man's a hundred?

STELLA That's right. Why?

SUSAN (*crossing to the double doors*) They never change, do they?

(SUSAN, *rubbing her bottom, exits by the double doors*)

JOAN. That's all I needed.
STELLA. What?
JOAN. To restore my sanity. Men!

(GEORGE *enters* R)

(*To George*) And that includes you.
GEORGE. What does?
JOAN. Skip it. Have you come to say good-bye?
GEORGE (*moving to the desk*) I have to ring Mr Elton first.
JOAN. That should be worth listening to.

(*The* NURSE *enters by the double doors, carrying a tray with two bottles of medicine, two glasses, and two spoons. She is wearing ordinary clothes, having discarded her uniform. She crosses to the door* L)

If you feel like giving them a lethal dose, we'll all testify that it was an accident.
STELLA. Joan!
NURSE. I would remind you, Miss Banstead, that I'm performing my very difficult duties only under protest. Your so-called humorous remarks do not help.

(*The* NURSE *taps on the door* L *and exits*)

JOAN. It's wonderful to see someone who's really happy in her work.

(*Raised voices are heard off* L)

STELLA. Now what?
JOAN. There's certainly never a dull moment around here.

(*A crash of glass is heard off* L)

STELLA. What was that?
JOAN. I'd say we're suddenly short of medicines.

(*The* NURSE *enters agitatedly* L)

STELLA. What is it, Nurse?
NURSE (*moving above the sofa*) He attacked me. With his stick. The stupid old fool! Does he imagine I've never seen a man without his trousers on before? Never in all my experience . . . Oh . . .
GEORGE. What's the matter?
NURSE (*moving* L) She wasn't there—Mrs Mellowes.
GEORGE. Not there?
STELLA. But she must be.
NURSE. She isn't.
JOAN. There's the bathroom.
NURSE. I went in there.
STELLA. But where else could she be?
GEORGE. Damn! If she's wandering about the hotel, she'll probably fall down the first staircase she comes to.

STELLA (*crossing to George*) Ask Henry where she is.
GEORGE (*crossing to the door* L) You get on to the hall porter.

(STELLA *lifts the telephone receiver.*
GEORGE *exits* L)

JOAN. Here we go again. (*She collects her camera*) Better be ready
for a picture, I suppose.
STELLA. Joan, please!
JOAN. Well, you never know. (*She crosses to the Nurse*) The old
man may have bumped her off and pushed her down the plughole.
STELLA (*into the telephone*) Hall porter, please . . .

(GEORGE *enters* L)

GEORGE. He says she's gone out.
JOAN. You mean out of the hotel?
GEORGE. That's what he says.
JOAN. Oh, Lord!
GEORGE. This would happen.
JOAN (*moving up* R) Where's she gone?
GEORGE. He doesn't know.
STELLA. But if she tries to cross a road . . . Oh, dear, why doesn't
he answer?
GEORGE (*crossing to* L *of Joan*) We don't even know if she can
find her way back. (*To the Nurse*) I don't know how you let this
happen.
NURSE. Me!
GEORGE. You're supposed to be looking after them, aren't you?
NURSE. Their health. I'm not their keeper.
GEORGE. What's the matter with that damn hall porter?
STELLA (*into the telephone*) Hall porter? . . . This is the penthouse
suite. Have you seen anything of Mrs Mellowes? . . . Yes, the old
lady from this suite . . . What time was that? . . . Did she mention
where she was going? . . . Very well . . . No, it's all right, thank you.
(*She replaces the receiver*) She left the hotel about an hour and a half
ago.
GEORGE. On her own?
STELLA. Apparently.
GEORGE. Didn't she tell anyone where she was off to?
STELLA. Not a word.

(HENRY, *fully dressed and carrying his stick, enters* L)

GEORGE. Oh Lord! (*He crosses to Henry*) Mr Mellowes, do try
and think. Didn't she say anything at all about where she was
going?
HENRY. Who?
GEORGE. Your wife, of course.
HENRY. Here, you don't have to shout. I'm not deaf.
GEORGE. But did she?

HENRY. Did she what? Speak up.

GEORGE. Say where she was going?

HENRY. I don't remember.

STELLA. Please, Mr Mellowes, do try.

HENRY. I'm sorry, missy. I'm getting on, you see . . .

GEORGE. Oh, my God! (*He crosses to* L *of Joan*) Look, we've got to find her before something happens to her.

STELLA. How can we? She could be anywhere.

GEORGE. We've got to try. If she's on foot, she can't have got far at her pace even in an hour and a half. We'll each get a taxi and scour the streets. Come on.

(JOAN *and* STELLA *move to the double doors*)

Nurse, you keep an eye on him. Oh, if you see my wife, say I shan't be long.

NURSE. Very well.

(JOAN *and* STELLA *exit by the double doors*)

GEORGE. And don't let him out of your sight for an instant. If he gives you any trouble, tie him up.

(GEORGE *exits by the double doors.* HENRY *laboriously lowers himself on to the sofa, at the left end of it, grunting and muttering*)

NURSE (*moving to* R *of the sofa*) Did you say something, Mr Mellowes?

HENRY. No, I didn't. Dashing about! They're all mad here, if you ask me.

(*The* NURSE *collects some knitting from behind the cushion at the right end of the sofa, then seats herself* R *of Henry on the sofa, close to him*)

Ugh! (*He examines the sharp crease in his trousers*) Making me look like some pansy, that's what they're a doing of. (*He pauses*) I said they're making me look like a pansy. (*He pauses*) You lost your tongue?

NURSE (*knitting*) I heard you.

HENRY. Oh!

(HENRY *watches the* NURSE *as she knits rapidly*)

You're in a powerful hurry with that there knitting. You expecting a little one?

NURSE. Oh!

HENRY. Well, are you?

NURSE. I'm not married.

HENRY. Ah, they tell me there's a lot of it goes on nowadays.

NURSE. You stupid old man!

HENRY. Here, you mind what you're a saying of.

NURSE. This happens to be a sweater.

HENRY. Go on! Little devil's going to look funny in a sweater, isn't he?

(*There is a knock at the double doors*)

NURSE (*calling*) Yes? Come in?

(GEOFFREY WALLCOTT-BROWN, *a B.B.C. interviewer, enters by the double doors. He is young, slightly built, and gushing. He wears casual clothes and carries a portable battery-operated tape-recorder*)

GEOFFREY. Oh, 'morning. (*He puts the recorder on the table* RC) Mr Maxwell here? He is expecting me.

NURSE. He's had to go out.

GEOFFREY. Will he be long? (*He moves to* R *of the sofa*) I'm Geoffrey Wallcot-Brown. B.B.C., you know. It's about the recording. Oh, of course, you two must be Mr and Mrs Mellowes. How do you do? I must congratulate you. Really, Mrs Mellowes, you don't look anything like a hundred. Seventy at the most.

(HENRY *is convulsed. Laughing wildly, he rocks back and forth, lifting his stick and bringing it down repeatedly on the floor as he raises his feet. The* NURSE *rises and backs* GEOFFREY RC)

What did I say?

NURSE. I happen to be the nurse. And, for your information, I'm not yet fifty.

GEOFFREY (*moving down* R) Oh, Lord!

NURSE (*moving to* R *of the sofa*) Mr Mellowes, stop that stupid laughing at once.

HENRY. Seventy at the most! (*He brings his feet and his stick down and the stick slips from his grasp. He loses his balance and topples on the floor*)

NURSE (*darting to Henry*) You would do a thing like that. Here, let me help you up.

HENRY. I'll get meself up.

NURSE. Do as I tell you.

HENRY (*thrusting aside her helping hand*) I got down myself, I'll get up myself.

NURSE. Oh, very well.

HENRY. Where's me stick?

(*The* NURSE *hands Henry his stick*)

NURSE. Have you hurt yourself?

HENRY. Stop bothering me, can't you? (*He struggles to his feet but cannot straighten his back*) Ooh!

NURSE. What is it?

HENRY. Me back! Me back's gone again.

NURSE. Whereabouts? Show me.

HENRY (*indicating with his hand*) Right there.

NURSE (*prodding him*) There?

HENRY. Ooh! You clumsy great elephant.

NURSE (*grasping Henry*) Back towards the sofa.

HENRY. I can't.

NURSE. Then stand still while I massage your back. (*She massages Henry's back*)

(HENRY *practically leaps in the air*)

HENRY. Ooh! Let go of me. Let go. You got hands like bulldozers.

(SARAH, *wearing hat and coat, enters by the double doors*)

NURSE. I'm only trying to help you. If you'd only back into the sofa, I could do something.

SARAH (*moving to R of the sofa*) What's going on here?

HENRY. It's me back, Sarah. I got fixed again.

NURSE. He won't do what he's told.

SARAH. That's nothing new. (*She pushes the Nurse aside to RC*) Out of me way.

NURSE. You see, if he'd back into the sofa . . .

SARAH. Henry, stop hopping about.

HENRY. I'm fixed, I tell you.

(SARAH *swings her handbag and hits* HENRY *in the pit of his back. He lets out a yell but straightens and is upright again*)

NURSE. Mrs Mellowes! You might have done him a serious injury.

SARAH. Oh! Well, you didn't seem to be getting nowhere. Better now, Henry?

HENRY (*sitting on the sofa, at the left end of it*) Yes, yes, I reckon so.

NURSE (*to Sarah*) I suppose you know everybody's out searching for you. Where have you been?

SARAH. Out.

(*The* NURSE *crosses to the telephone*)

NURSE (*lifting the receiver*) Very well. (*Into the telephone*) Give me the hall porter, please . . .

GEOFFREY (*crossing to Sarah; uncomfortably*) I gather this is Mrs Mellowes. I'm terribly sorry.

NURSE (*into the telephone*) Hall porter? . . . Have you seen Mr Maxwell and the two young ladies? . . . Well, see if you can call them back. Say that Mrs Mellowes has returned. (*She replaces the receiver*)

(SARAH *removes her coat.* GEOFFREY *hastens to assist her*)

SARAH. And who might you be?

GEOFFREY. I'm from the B.B.C. I've come to make the recording for radio newsreel.

SARAH. Oh? I thought me and Henry was going to make it.

GEOFFREY. You are, you are.

SARAH. Then why did you say you were going to do it? (*She sits R of Henry on the sofa*)

GEOFFREY (*moving up* R) I didn't mean that.

NURSE (*moving to Geoffrey and taking Sarah's coat from him*) You don't know what you're in for. As for you, Mrs Mellowes—(*she moves to* R *of the sofa*) you have quite a lot of explaining to do.

SARAH. Not to you, I haven't.

NURSE (*crossing above the sofa to the door* L) We'll see about that.

GEOFFREY (*to the Nurse*) I do apologize about just now. Naturally, I can see the difference. I mean, well, side by side.

(*The* NURSE *gives Geoffrey a withering look and exits* L *with Sarah's coat*)

(*He mops his brow*) When I let go a clanger, it really clangs. (*He moves down* R)

HENRY. Where you been, Sarah?

SARAH. Wouldn't you like to know!

GEOFFREY (*moving* C) Ah, you still have secrets from one another. How absolutely charming. Honestly, I think you're both quite fabulous. You know, I've never met a centenarian before. And here I am with two of them. It's quite exciting, isn't it? Have you ever made a recording before? Of course you haven't. Never mind, it's all quite simple. At least, it is usually. I tell you what, while we're waiting for Mr Maxwell, we could have a little rehearsal. Shall we?

SARAH. Suit yourself.

GEOFFREY. Good. (*He moves to the recorder and uncoils the microphone*) I won't switch on, of course. You speak into this microphone.

SARAH. What do we have to say?

HENRY (*rising*) I got a bit of paper somewhere.

GEOFFREY. No, that's for later. (*He moves* C *with the microphone*) I'll just ask you a few simple questions. Now, let me see. Yes, I know.

(HENRY *crosses and sits in the armchair* C. GEOFFREY *transfers the microphone from his own mouth to the mouths of the others as the text requires*)

Mr Mellowes——

(HENRY *burps*)

—though people are living longer today, very few achieve the century. To what do you attribute your longevity?

HENRY. My long what?

SARAH. Henry! You mind what you say. We don't want none of your coarse remarks coming out of the wireless.

HENRY. Now, see here, Sarah . . .

GEOFFREY. Never mind. Never mind. Let's forget it. I know. Mrs Mellowes, I expect you have lots of grandchildren.

SARAH. Aye, there's twenty-four on 'em.

HENRY. Twenty-three, you mean.

SARAH. Twenty-four. I counted 'em up only the other day.

GEOFFREY (*moving up* C) Oh, no!

SARAH. Trouble with him is he's past it.

HENRY. Past it, am I?

SARAH. You can't even remember what year it is.

HENRY. I can remember how many grandchildren we got and it's only twenty-three.

GEOFFREY. Let's calm down, shall we?

(*The* NURSE *enters* L *and crosses to* L *of Geoffrey*)

Oh, Nurse, could you spare a minute?

SARAH. I can name every one of them.

HENRY. Then let's hear you.

SARAH. The first was Harold.

HENRY. No, it weren't.

GEOFFREY (*moving down* C) I say, what lovely weather we're having, aren't we, Nurse? (*To Sarah*) So nice for your stay here. It must be quite an experience for you, what with one thing and another.

SARAH. Be quiet when I'm talking.

(GEOFFREY *moves up* C)

(*To Henry*) Course it were Harold.

HENRY. It were not.

GEOFFREY. Oh, Lord, they don't teach you about this sort of thing at the B.B.C.

(GEORGE *enters by the double doors*)

GEORGE (*moving to* R *of Geoffrey*) Oh, Mr Wallcot-Brown, sorry about this. (*He crosses to* R *of the sofa*) Mrs Mellowes, where do you think you've been? We were on the point of sending out search parties for you.

SARAH. More fool you. I wasn't lost.

GEORGE. Where were you?

SARAH. That's my business.

GEORGE (*moving to the window*) You mustn't do things like that.

SARAH. I'll do as I please, and you remember that, young man.

(STELLA *and* JOAN *enter by the double doors.* JOAN *moves to the desk and sits at it*)

STELLA (*crossing to* R *of the sofa*) Thank goodness! Are you all right, Mrs Mellowes?

SARAH. 'Course I am, dear. You don't have to worry about me.

HENRY. It weren't Harold. It were Henry after me.

GEOFFREY (*moving above the table* RC) Oh, Lord, don't let them start that again. I wonder if we might get on with the recording. I've been having rather a difficult time.

JOAN. We can imagine.

GEORGE. Oh, this is Miss Haley—and Miss Banstead.
GEOFFREY. How do you do?
GEORGE. Nurse you've met already.
NURSE. We've had that pleasure.

(*The* NURSE *exits by the double doors*)

GEORGE. Let's get started, shall we? Where are those questions and answers?
STELLA. Here. (*She crosses to the desk, collects three copies of the broadcast and hands one each to Henry, Sarah and Geoffrey*)

(JOAN *rises, crosses and sits on the window-seat.* STELLA *sits at the desk*)

GEORGE. You understand, both of you? You listen to the questions and then give the answers typed out on your paper. That clear?
HENRY. Aye.
GEORGE. Good. (*To Geoffrey*) Over to you.
GEOFFREY. Thank you. (*He switches on the tape-recorder and moves* C, *microphone in hand. Into the microphone*) This is Geoffrey Wallcot-Brown's interview with Mr and Mrs Mellowes in the penthouse suite of the *Royal Park Hotel*. Cue material follows. Mr and Mrs Mellowes are staying here as the guests of the readers of the *County Gazette* to celebrate their hundredth birthdays and the eightieth anniversary of their marriage. I shall go ahead in five seconds from now. (*He pauses*)

(HENRY *sneezes*)

Mrs Mellowes, nowadays, when marriage is treated as something one can get out of at any time, the example set by you and your husband is truly impressive. May I say that when you and Mr Mellowes first met, all those years ago, it was love at first sight? (*He transfers the microphone to Sarah*)
SARAH (*reading*) Yes, it was. I can still remember . . .
HENRY. Love at first sight! What—us?
GEORGE. Mr Mellowes!
HENRY. Why, she turned me down five times.
STELLA. Mr Mellowes, please!
HENRY. Only I was fool enough to ask her a sixth time.
GEORGE. Cut it out!
HENRY. It's true.
GEORGE. I don't care if it is true.

(GEOFFREY, *bemused, switches the microphone from mouth to mouth*)

HENRY. You ask her about Bob Taylor.
GEORGE. Who the devil's he?
HENRY. My cousin, as lived over at Lowestoft. Exmouth.
SARAH. Now, there was a man. My Bob, bless him! Giant of a

man, he was. A sailor with blue eyes that fair melted your heart. I
loved that boy, loved him with all my girlish heart.

GEORGE (*crossing down* L; *to Geoffrey*) Good God, man, turn that
thing off.

GEOFFREY. Oh, Lord, yes! (*He moves to the table* RC *and switches off
the recorder*)

SARAH. He'd have been sitting here with me now, only his ship
went down and him with it.

HENRY. Aye, he didn't know but that were his lucky day.

GEORGE (*crossing below the sofa to* C) Stop saying things like that.
(*To Geoffrey*) I'm sorry, but we'll have to call this off.

GEOFFREY (*packing up the recorder*) I'm already on my way out.
This is dynamite.

GEORGE (*moving to Geoffrey*) I don't know how much you re-
corded . . .

GEOFFREY. We'll clean it off, never you worry. (*He picks up the
recorder*)

GEORGE. I dare say you can cook up some excuse for the B.B.C.

GEOFFREY. Leave it to me. (*He moves to the double doors*) My God,
imagine if this had been live. They'd think we were trying to bring
back satire. The phones at Broadcasting House would never stop
ringing.

(GEOFFREY *exits by the double doors*)

GEORGE. You two old reprobates. (*He moves down* C) What do you
mean by behaving like that?

(SARAH *takes out a handkerchief and dabs her eyes*)

(*He moves to* R *of the sofa*) Oh, look, I'm sorry if I shouted at you.

SARAH. It wasn't that. It was him—mentioning my Bob.

HENRY. She's off.

SARAH. I only saw my Bob just once in six months of marriage.

GEORGE. In six months of what?

SARAH. We'd only been married six months when his ship went
down.

GEORGE (*moving up* C) Oh, no!

STELLA (*rising and crossing to* R *of the sofa*) You mean you've been
married before?

SARAH. Yes, dear, just for a little while.

GEORGE. You never told us.

SARAH. You never asked.

GEORGE (*moving above the table* RC; *to Henry*) Is this true?

HENRY. Aye, she married Bob Taylor first. Always preferred him
to me. Bounder he was, too.

STELLA. But when was this?

SARAH. I was sixteen, dear. At sixteen and a half I was a widow.

GEORGE. Sixteen and a half. It's all right. They've still been
married eighty years.

SARAH. Well, of course we have. And I ought to know how many long weary years it's been.

GEORGE. Does anyone else know of this earlier marriage?

SARAH. Well, I got two daughters left. The one we lives with and the married one at Bournemouth. They know.

GEORGE. They aren't likely to talk. Well, thank Heaven, it needn't make any difference.

JOAN. Saved again!

GEORGE. Look, you two, there's no need for Mr Elton to learn about this.

JOAN. Might be worth it, just to see his face.

GEORGE. Don't you dare! He isn't to know she went out on her own, either. (*To Sarah*) Where was it you went?

SARAH. I went to Wimbledon, if you must know.

GEORGE. Why Wimbledon?

STELLA. Do you know someone there?

SARAH. It was a solemn duty, dear. I went to put some flowers on my first husband's grave.

GEORGE. His grave?

(STELLA *moves above the sofa*)

JOAN (*rising*) I thought you said he was lost at sea.

SARAH. So he was.

GEORGE. Oh, I see. (*He moves* C) They recovered his body.

SARAH. Yes, that's right. Some natives, it was. They thought he was dead at first. He lived with them for five years.

HENRY. And we didn't see him again for another five. Kept out of sight, he did. Only come back when he knew she'd married me. Talk about a dirty trick!

GEORGE. Are you telling me that you and Mrs Mellowes . . . Good God!

HENRY. Had another wife by then, he had. Australian girl. Lovely, she was, too. No wonder he let us all believe he was drowned.

GEORGE. I don't believe it.

JOAN. I do.

STELLA. Mrs. Mellowes, is it true what you've said?

SARAH. Every word of it.

GEORGE (*moving down* C) But this means you two aren't married.

SARAH. 'Course we were married. In church, too.

GEORGE. I know that. I checked. But it wasn't legal.

JOAN (*crossing and sitting in the armchair* RC) How do you like that! We've got the readers of the *Gazette* to put up their money to celebrate eighty years of bigamy.

HENRY. What's that?

STELLA. The ceremony wasn't legal.

GEORGE. In any case you should have waited seven years.

HENRY. Seven years?

GEORGE. It's the law. (*To Sarah*) Does anyone know where you've been?
SARAH. No.
GEORGE. Heaven be praised for that.
SARAH. Oh, except the young man.
GEORGE (*moving to R of the sofa*) What young man?
SARAH. The one as gave me a lift in his car.
GEORGE. What! Who was he?
SARAH. I don't know. He come up to me downstairs and said could he take me somewhere.
GEORGE. Did he give his name?
SARAH. No. He works on a newspaper, though.
GEORGE. Good God! Which?
SARAH. He didn't say.
JOAN (*rising and moving R*) Well, I'd say that just about winds us all up.
GEORGE. Did you tell him what you've told us?
SARAH. I'm not exactly sure. He asked a lot of questions.
GEORGE. Did he go with you into the cemetery?
SARAH. Yes. Very sympathetic he was and all.
JOAN (*moving up R*) Then we can take it he knows the lot.
STELLA. What was he like?
SARAH. I didn't really notice. Short, dark.
GEORGE (*moving up C*) Hell!
JOAN (*moving to R of George*) Are you still leaving us, George?
GEORGE. I don't know. I hadn't counted on this.
JOAN. Well, start counting.

(HENRY *has dropped off and snores.* JOAN *moves to* HENRY, *gives him a dig and he wakes*)

Yes, you can doze off now.
HENRY. What's that?
JOAN. It's a pity you weren't as dozy as this eighty years ago.
GEORGE. If only we knew who it was she spoke to.
JOAN. I'll lay any money it's the *Courier*.
GEORGE. If it is, they'll make the most of it. They know Miss Jessop. They know her views and the charitable work she does. If they print this, she'll be made to look so ridiculous, she'll never be able to hold up her head in the town again. She certainly couldn't go on running the *Gazette*.
STELLA (*moving up C*) And if the *Courier* were to make her another offer . . .
GEORGE (*moving to the desk*) Don't, please! There's nothing for it. I'll have to tell Mr Elton.
JOAN. Not yet.
GEORGE. He'll have to handle this.
JOAN. Maybe, but not yet. I'll go down and see if I can find out anything. Perhaps this fellow's still here.

GEORGE. Supposing he is?
JOAN. We could talk to him.
GEORGE. A lot of good that would do.
JOAN. You want me to go and see?
GEORGE. I suppose so. (*He sits at the desk*)

(HENRY *snores*)

Oh, for Pete's sake!
SARAH. Henry! Wake up, you old fool.
JOAN. What about their programme now?
GEORGE (*rising*) The House of Commons.
JOAN. Honoured guests at a luncheon to be given by Sir Rupert Hoxon, M.P.
GEORGE. They won't even get past the soup.
STELLA. But we can't call it off now.
GEORGE. After what we know.
JOAN. Oh, come, George, if you're going to make sexual rectitude a condition of lunching at the Commons, where will the M.P.s go?
GEORGE (*sitting at the desk*) I've got to think.
JOAN. While you're thinking, I'll go and take a look downstairs. And if you take my advice, you won't tell the old man till we're absolutely forced to.

(JOAN *exits by the double doors*)

STELLA (*moving above the table* RC) She's right, George. After all, you've got out of worse scrapes than this one.
GEORGE. You call this a scrape? In about an hour from now she'll probably be imparting all these grisly details to Sir Rupert Hoxon. He'll probably choke to death over the entree.
STELLA (*moving to* L *of George*) George, pull yourself together.
GEORGE. And what about tonight? Those two are the guests of honour at a dinner given by the Marriage Guidance Council.
STELLA. We'll just have to chance it. There's nothing else to do. (*She crosses to* R *of the sofa*) You won't breathe a word of what's happened, will you, Mrs Mellowes?
SARAH. Why should I?
GEORGE. You'd better not, because if you do . . . (*He rises and moves* RC) My God! I've just realized; bigamy is a criminal offence. You two could be sent to prison for seven years.
STELLA. At their age?
GEORGE. I've never heard of an age limit for criminal offences. Not that he'd care. He'd be asleep for six years out of the seven. Wake him up, for Pete's sake.
STELLA. Oh, dear. Mr Mellowes, do wake up.
SARAH. You can imagine what a jolly life I have.
HENRY (*waking*) Oh, it's you, my dear.
STELLA. It's time to get ready. Let me help you.

HENRY (*rising*) Must have dropped off. All this gadding about, you know.

STELLA (*leading Henry to the door* L) You can have a rest before we leave. Come along, now. You, too, Mrs Mellowes.

GEORGE. And, remember, not a word about what's happened this morning.

SARAH. You sure about what you said—me and Henry not being man and wife?

GEORGE (*moving up* R) I wish I wasn't. Surely you knew?

SARAH. Maybe we did. I can't remember. It's a terrible long time ago.

STELLA. Don't let it worry you, Mrs Mellowes.

SARAH. I'm not. What's bothering me is thinking of all the times I wanted to leave him and didn't.

HENRY. What about me? I been supporting you for eighty years and I didn't have to. Darn particular she were, and all. Nothing but the best. Spent money like water, that woman did.

(HENRY *exits* L. STELLA *closes the door behind him*)

SARAH. Chance would have been a fine thing.

STELLA (*moving to* L *of the sofa*) How can you say such things to one another?

SARAH. I'm sorry, dear. I dare say we've been a bit of a shock to you. But you wait till you've been married to the same man for eighty years.

STELLA (*sitting* L *of Sarah on the sofa*) But you must have loved him once.

SARAH. I expect I did. He wasn't a bad man in his way. He's been mean and jealous; he's always kept me short of money; he made me work like I was his slave; and one time he used to beat me regular. I forget how many times he was unfaithful. But he wasn't worse nor any other husband. Yes, I reckon I must have loved the old devil for a year or so.

STELLA (*rising and moving down* L) A year or so!

SARAH. You got to face it, dear. It don't take more'n about a year to get to know a husband—what there is to know. (*She rises and crosses to the door* L) One year and you know what they're going to do and say for the rest of their lives.

(STELLA *moves to* R *of Sarah*)

You know every expression on their silly faces and every thought in their heads. There's no getting away from it, dear—men is terrible bores.

GEORGE. For a bridegroom of one day I find that a message of hope and encouragement. (*To Stella*) If I'm not here when you come back, look for my body on the pavement down there.

STELLA. Wait till I get back and I'll probably jump with you. Come on, Mrs Mellowes.

SARAH. I hope they give us something nice to eat at this here luncheon. Going out has given me quite an appetite.

(SARAH *and* STELLA *exit* L.
GEORGE *sinks wearily into the armchair* C.
BRENDA *enters* R, *wearing her hat and coat*)

GEORGE. Brenda! (*He rises and moves* C) Oh, Lord, I'd forgotten.
BRENDA. Forgotten what?
GEORGE. Look, Brenda, I'm sorry, terribly sorry. There's another crisis. A serious one. I can't come.
BRENDA. You can't come! (*She moves up* C)
GEORGE. Now, wait. (*He moves to her*) Let me explain.
BRENDA. Don't touch me.
GEORGE. Please. Hear what I have to say.
BRENDA. Keep away from me.
GEORGE. But you don't understand. I can't walk out and leave them to it. It's my responsibility.
BRENDA. I thought I was your responsibility now.
GEORGE. Darling, I know how you feel. But I must stay. Only till tomorrow night then it'll all be over.
BRENDA. Tomorrow night! You expect me to hang around here, watching you make a fool of yourself, till tomorrow night? Oh, no.
GEORGE. I wish you wouldn't talk to me like that. Anyway, I have to stay.
BRENDA. Well, I haven't. (*She moves to the double doors*) I'm leaving for my flat and I'm leaving now.
GEORGE. Brenda, please!
BRENDA. Are you coming or aren't you?
GEORGE. I can't.
BRENDA. Is that your final choice?
GEORGE. My *final* choice?
BRENDA. That's what I said.
GEORGE. Darling, be sensible.
BRENDA. Come or don't come. It's up to you.
GEORGE. I can't. (*He moves above the sofa*) I'll ring you as soon as I can.
BRENDA. Then let's hope I'm still there to answer. (*She opens the door*)
GEORGE (*moving to her*) Brenda!

(BRENDA *exits by the double doors, closing them behind her*)

(*He moves to the bar*) Oh, damn, damn, damn!

(STELLA *enters* L *and crosses to George*)

STELLA. George, you'd better come.
GEORGE. Are they fighting again?
STELLA. I wish they were. You'll never believe what's happening now.

GEORGE. Yes, I will. (*He moves to the desk*) After what I've gone through, I'll believe anything. (*Anxiously*) What is it?

STELLA (*moving down* c) You know they have a daughter at Bournemouth? Well, she's going there. She's packing.

GEORGE. Packing?

STELLA. He said she was a kept woman, so she's leaving him.

GEORGE. What! (*He moves to* R *of Stella*) Tell him he must stop her.

STELLA (*hysterically*) Him! He couldn't be more pleased. He's helping her with her packing.

GEORGE *crosses quickly to the door* L *as—*

the CURTAIN *falls*

ACT III

Scene i

Scene—*The same. About 10 p.m. the same evening.*

When the Curtain *rises, the lights are on and the window curtains are closed.* Stella *is seated at the desk, typing. The telephone rings.* Stella *lifts the receiver.*

Stella (*into the telephone*) Penthouse suite . . . No, he isn't back from the Marriage Guidance Council dinner yet . . . Any minute. I should think . . . To the manager's office . . . Yes, certainly. (*She replaces the receiver, yawns and stretches*)

(*Voices are heard off*)

Sarah (*off*) And I say you did.

(George *enters by the double doors. He is followed on by* Sarah, Henry *and* Joan. *All are wearing outdoor clothes.* George *looks tired and exasperated.* Sarah *crosses below the sofa.* Henry *moves* c. George *stands up* c *and* Joan *stands up* r)

Henry. It's a lie. I heard every word of his speech.

Sarah. You was snoring right through it.

George. Cut it out, can't you?

Sarah (*sitting on the sofa*) Not that I blame you. Load of rubbish, it were. Beats me why they ever made him a bishop.

George. Will you shut up? The place for you is bed. (*To* Joan) Where's Nurse?

Joan. Coming. (*She sits in the armchair* RC)

Stella. Was everything all right?

George. Oh, perfect. She told the bishop she thought marriage licences should be renewable every year like a wireless licence— so that if you don't like what you're getting you needn't renew it.

Stella. Oh, no!

Sarah. Aye, imagine how thoughtful and attentive husbands would get as the end of the year come round. Nothing would be too good for the little woman then.

George (*moving to* R *of the sofa*) You're a disruptive influence, that's what you are. A menace to society. Come along—bed.

Sarah. I'm not tired.

(Henry *sinks into the chair* c)

George. Now, see here . . .

Sarah. I'm not tired, I said.

GEORGE (*crossing above the sofa to* L *of it*) You must be. You haven't stopped talking for the last three hours. Even during the speeches we could hear you better than we could hear the speakers.

STELLA (*rising and moving to* R *of the sofa*) Mrs Mellowes, that was very naughty of you.

GEORGE. I doubt if the bishop will ever get over it.

SARAH. He swore at me, he did. Under his breath, but I heard him. Old fool, going on about the joys of married life and him never married. What's more, if you ask me, he mentioned a few things no unmarried bishop ought to know about.

GEORGE. Even so, there was no need for you to say so in a loud whisper that practically reverberated throughout the hall. (*He crosses to* L *of Henry*) And you were as bad. If you were compelled to tell the bishop that story about the nun and the bell-ringer, there was no need to add that you got the story from me.

(STELLA *moves above the sofa.*
The NURSE *enters by the double doors*)

Oh, there you are, Nurse. Get them to bed, will you?

NURSE (*crossing to* C) Very well. Come along now, both of you.

GEORGE. Anyone phoned, Stella?

STELLA. Mr Elton, for the fourth time. I assured him everything was going perfectly.

NURSE (*moving to Henry*) Up you get, Mr Mellowes.

HENRY. You keep your hands off me. I can get up myself.

NURSE. Very well.

GEORGE (*to Stella*) Any word from my wife?

STELLA. Sorry, George.

(GEORGE *crossed down* R)

NURSE (*moving to Sarah*) Mrs Mellowes . . .

SARAH. I'll go to bed when I'm ready.

NURSE. You'll go to bed now.

SARAH. Oh, and who's going to make me?

STELLA. Mrs Mellowes, please. We've all had a hard day. We're tired if you're not. (*She moves up* C)

SARAH. Well, perhaps I will turn in—but of my own free will, not because someone orders me to. (*Sharply*) Henry!

HENRY. What?

SARAH. Bed.

HENRY. I only just set down. (*Grumbling, he struggles to his feet*)

(*The* NURSE *crosses to the door* L)

STELLA (*moving above the table* RC) Oh, George, I nearly forgot: you're wanted in the manager's office.

GEORGE. What for?

STELLA. They didn't say.

GEORGE. You don't think they've found out about . . . (*He nods towards Sarah and Henry*)

STELLA. Of course not. It's probably some routine matter—about tomorrow's dinner perhaps.

GEORGE. I hope you're right.

(HENRY *crosses to the door* L *and staggers*)

Look out! You all right, Mr Mellowes?

(JOAN *rises and crosses to Henry to help him*)

HENRY. 'Course I am. (*He throws off Joan's helping hand*) Let go of me.

(JOAN *moves up* C)

NURSE. He's worn out, if you ask me. He should never have been brought here in the first place. Take it gently, now. (*She opens the door* L)

HENRY. Stop fussing me, woman. It's worse'n having two wives, that's what it is. Bloody women!

(HENRY, *muttering, exits* L)

NURSE. Mrs Mellowes.

SARAH. I'm coming.

(*The* NURSE *sighs and exits* L, *leaving the door open*)

What are we doing tomorrow?

STELLA (*moving to* R *of the sofa*) Nothing in the morning .You can have a nice lie-in. In the afternoon there's a trip on the Thames to the Tower.

SARAH. Aye, I've always wanted to go to the Tower.

STELLA (*moving above the sofa*) In the evening there's the farewell dinner. And you'll be the guests of honour, you and Mr Mellowes.

SARAH. Then I hope we have something nice to eat. Poor stuff they give us tonight. Wasn't cooked properly, neither.

GEORGE (*moving* RC) So you loudly informed the assembled gathering.

SARAH. Aye, that got quite a laugh, that did.

GEORGE. I happened to be sitting next to the Organizing Secretary. Look, go to bed, will you, please.

SARAH. What about tomorrow night? Have you told my daughter at Bournemouth she's to come and take me to her place?

GEORGE (*sitting in the armchair* RC) Well, no, not yet.

SARAH. You promised you would.

GEORGE. I know I did.

SARAH. I only stayed here because you promised.

JOAN (*moving to* R *of the sofa*) There's plenty of time.

SARAH. She needs warning. She'll have to get a room ready for me.

STELLA (*moving to* L *of the sofa*) But you can't really be serious about leaving Mr Mellowes.

SARAH. I'm staying till tomorrow night like you said. Not a day more.

GEORGE. But you'll cause such a scandal.

SARAH. I can't help that. Not after the things he said to me.

JOAN. Oh, but he didn't mean them.

SARAH. He did. Every word. I know him.

GEORGE. But if you clear off like that, people will want to know why.

SARAH. I'll tell them why.

(JOAN *moves up* R)

GEORGE. You can't. Bigamy is a serious offence.

SARAH. Ah, yes. Seven years in prison, you said.

GEORGE. It could be.

SARAH. That's the law?

GEORGE. Yes, it is.

SARAH (*rising*) Then tell me—seeing you know so much about the law, have they ever sent anyone a hundred years old to prison yet? (*She pauses*) Then they aren't likely to start now, are they? So do mind what you promised. (*She crosses to the door* L) Besides, you wouldn't want the readers of that there newspaper of yours to know you tried to make me go on living with a man as wasn't my husband, would you?

(SARAH, *chuckling, exits* L. STELLA *closes the door.* JOAN *moves to the table* RC *and picks up a newspaper*)

GEORGE. And someone asked me if she was in full possession of her faculties.

JOAN. Well, I didn't expect to see one of my pictures in a London evening. (*She reads*) "Mr and Mrs Mellowes arriving at the *Royal Park Hotel.*"

GEORGE. It'll only make things worse when the truth about those two comes out.

JOAN. We don't know if it will come out. (*She replaces the newspaper on the table*)

GEORGE. It will.

STELLA (*moving and perching on the back of the sofa*) But there hasn't been a word about it yet in any paper. Not even in the *Courier.*

JOAN. I'm beginning to wonder if the old dear got confused about the whole thing.

GEORGE. Not her! She doesn't get that confused.

STELLA. But something would have appeared by now. What possible reason could they have for holding back?

GEORGE. I'll give you one possible reason. Tomorrow night we have the farewell dinner. There'll be a speech from Mr Elton, the presentations, the message from the Queen. On Monday the *Gazette* will feature it all on the front page—with more of your damn pictures. And the same morning out will come the *Courier*—or whoever it is—with the truth—also, no doubt, with pictures.

JOAN. Well, well, what a change we have here. (*She moves to the bar*) What's happened to the laughing carefree George we used to know?

GEORGE. Do you mind!

STELLA. George, hadn't you better go and see the manager? They said it was urgent.

GEORGE. Urgent? (*He rises and moves to the double doors*) Perhaps they have found out, then. You two had better hang around in case.

JOAN. We're not going anywhere. I need a good strong drink. How about you?

GEORGE. Later.

(GEORGE *exits by the double doors*)

JOAN (*pouring a drink for herself*) Stella?

STELLA. Please. Gin and something. Poor George!

JOAN. I don't know. Might do him good. Where's the whisky? (*She pours a drink for Stella*)

STELLA. Isn't it there?

JOAN. Can't see it.

STELLA. Joan, what did you mean about all this being good for George?

(JOAN *hands a drink to Stella, then takes her own drink and sits in the armchair* C)

JOAN. It's time George grew up. He's danced gaily through life, acting first and thinking afterwards. All very nice for him. And I admit there's never a dull moment when he's on a story. Still, the wear and tear on the rest of us can get pretty heavy. Maybe this will mature him. This and his marriage. And has he put his foot in it there. (*She raises her glass*) Cheers! (*She drinks*) It still baffles me why she married him. She usually stops short of marriage.

STELLA (*rising and moving* C) Joan! Have you been making enquiries about her?

JOAN. Matter of fact, I have—from a pal in Fleet Street.

STELLA. You shouldn't. It's no concern of ours.

JOAN. I know it isn't. But she's going to make him so wretchedly unhappy. We've worked together a lot—George and I—and I know him.

STELLA (*crossing and sitting on the desk chair*) There's nothing we can do.

JOAN. How could he have been so blind?

STELLA. Joan, stop it.

JOAN. Anyone but George would have seen at once . . .

STELLA. Stop it, Joan. Stop tormenting yourself.

JOAN. What did you say?

STELLA. Nothing. (*She rises*) I think I'll turn in.

JOAN. Stop tormenting myself. (*She rises*) Is that what you said?

STELLA. It slipped out. I'm sorry. I really am, Joan.

JOAN (*moving* c) Do I give myself away that much?

STELLA. Let's not talk about it.

JOAN. Does anyone else suspect?

STELLA. I don't think so.

JOAN. And George?

STELLA. Oh, no. He believes all those wisecracks you've been hiding behind.

JOAN. But they didn't fool you. (*She moves up* c *and sits on the stool*) I'm going to have to watch myself.

STELLA (*moving to Joan*) I'm sorry, Joan.

JOAN. Yes, I certainly am a lousy picker. First, my husband— a rotten little rat any teenager should have seen through; then a man who doesn't even notice I exist. And I'm criticizing George for choosing badly. That's a laugh. Never mind. After watching the antics of those two senile turtle doves in there, I'm thinking of giving up the whole idea, anyway.

(SUSAN *enters by the double doors, carrying a small bottle of pills*)

STELLA. Yes, Susan?

SUSAN. Nurse telephoned for these.

STELLA (*indicating the door* L) In there. (*She sits* R *of Joan on the bar stool*)

(SUSAN *crosses and exits* L)

Did you notice?

JOAN. Notice what?

STELLA. She's been crying.

JOAN. Yes, she's been dismissed. Didn't I tell you?

STELLA. No. Why? What's she done?

JOAN. Nothing. We had quite a chat. She believes someone's been scheming to get her thrown out.

STELLA. Does she know who?

JOAN. If she does, she won't say.

(SUSAN *enters* L *and moves up* c)

SUSAN. It's Mrs Mellowes. She's rather excited. Nurse is giving her some sleeping pills.

JOAN. That's something the old man will never need.

SUSAN (*crossing to the double doors*) Good night, then.

JOAN. Good night.

STELLA. Good night, Susan.

(SUSAN *exits by the double doors*)

JOAN. It wouldn't surprise me if it's Scott who got her the sack.

STELLA. Scott?

JOAN. I'm certain there's something between them. It's the sort of thing he'd do if she'd become an embarrassment.

(*The* NURSE *enters* L)

STELLA. Everything all right, Nurse?
NURSE. They're both over-tired. (*She moves above the sofa*) I advise you to let them down lightly tomorrow. But of course you won't.
JOAN. Have a drink, Nurse.
NURSE (*crossing to the double doors*) No, thank you.
STELLA. We're sorry you're having such a difficult time.
NURSE. I've had a difficult time all my life. I don't expect it to change now.

(*The* NURSE *exits by the double doors*)

JOAN. It's hard, but there's nothing so unattractive as a worthy woman.

(GEORGE *enters by the double doors and moves* RC)

STELLA (*rising and moving to* R *of George*) What happened?
JOAN (*rising*) Was it about those two old frauds in there?
GEORGE. No, it wasn't.
STELLA. That's a relief. Well, I'm off to bed.
GEORGE. Not yet.
JOAN (*moving to* L *of George*) What is it, George?
GEORGE (*picking up the newspaper from the table* RC) They wanted to see me about this picture.
JOAN. My one—of the old couple?
GEORGE. I can hardly believe it even now.
STELLA. Believe what?
GEORGE. The police are downstairs.
JOAN. The police?
STELLA. Because of this picture?
JOAN. You can't mean they've found out they're bigamists?
GEORGE. No, not that.
STELLA. Then what, for heaven's sake?
GEORGE. I'm not supposed to talk about it.
JOAN. Do you want to drive us mad? Let's have it.
GEORGE. You promise you won't breathe a word?
JOAN. Yes, yes.
STELLA. Of course.
GEORGE. I mean it.
JOAN. All right, all right.
GEORGE. Well, about an hour after that came out, a woman went to Scotland Yard. You've got a number of people in the background. She recognized one of them. Got a packet of money out of her, pretending to take her into business, then disappeared.
JOAN (*scrutinizing the picture*) You can't mean Scott!
GEORGE. Yes.

STELLA. No! Let me see. (*She takes the paper and looks at the picture*)

JOAN. Well, well!

GEORGE. Seems he's done quite a lot of it.

JOAN. Are they sure he's the man?

GEORGE. The woman is—quite positive.

STELLA. But it doesn't make sense. He must have a very good job here. (*She puts the paper on the table* RC)

GEORGE. He hadn't then. Incidentally, he got it by means of forged references. I imagine he only regards it as a stop-gap between more remunerative adventures.

JOAN. Yes, I doubt if regular work would have much appeal for him.

STELLA (*crossing to the desk*) It's still hard to believe.

JOAN (*moving up* c) Not to me. It fits somehow. Have they arrested him?

GEORGE. He's out. They're waiting till he gets back.

JOAN. George! Have you realized?

GEORGE. What?

JOAN. This will be a scoop for the *Gazette*. My picture! *Gazette* picture leads to arrest of well-known con man. How do you like that? We ought to get on to the office.

GEORGE. Not yet. I told you: it's confidential.

JOAN. Lord, yes! (*She moves down* L) We mustn't do anything to tip him off. Is that smoothie going to get a shock when he walks in tonight?

GEORGE. Why all this gloating? (*He moves* c) What's it to you?

JOAN. You wouldn't understand.

GEORGE. Try me.

JOAN. Let's put it this way. (*She crosses to* RC) I don't mind the gradual approach from a man. In its way it's flattering and reassuring. But I object to being treated as if I were a packet of instant sex. (*She picks up the newspaper*) George, what if Scott has already seen this? He's no fool. He might have decided to clear out just in case.

GEORGE. His things are still in his room.

JOAN. All of them?

GEORGE. I wouldn't know.

JOAN (*replacing the paper on the table*) He's clever enough to leave some behind to delay the pursuit. Just a minute! That maid, Susan. I wonder if that's the real reason she's been crying. Because she knows he's gone, I mean. (*She moves to the double doors*) I'm going to have a word with her.

GEORGE. You can't. (*He moves to* Joan) I'm not supposed to have told you.

JOAN. Don't worry. I know what to say.

(SARAH *enters* L. *She is wearing her dressing-gown and carries a visiting card*)

SARAH. Oh, there you are.

(GEORGE *moves and stands above the left end of the sofa.* JOAN *follows and stands above the right end of the sofa*)

STELLA (*moving to* R *of the sofa*) Is anything the matter?

SARAH (*moving to* L *of the sofa*) I found this in my handbag. I quite forgot he give it to me.

STELLA. What is it?

SARAH (*moving below the sofa and handing the card to Stella*) It's his card. That young fellow who drove me to the cemetery.

GEORGE (*moving to* R *of Stella*) Good God, let me have that. (*He takes the card*)

JOAN (*crossing to* RC) Well?

(GEORGE *hands the card to* JOAN, *who crosses and hands it to Stella*)

SARAH. Well, are Henry and me going to be exposed?

GEORGE. No, no, nothing of the sort. You can go back to bed and sleep in peace.

SARAH. Well, that's a relief. Not that I mind for myself. But I been thinking about my two daughters. It wouldn't be nice for them, would it?

GEORGE. Don't worry. Everything's going to be all right.

SARAH. Sure?

GEORGE. Quite sure.

SARAH. Oh! (*She moves to the door* L) Well, good night, then.

JOAN. Good night.

GEORGE. Good night, Mrs Mellowes. (*He crosses to Sarah*) Don't worry about a thing.

(SARAH *exits* L. GEORGE *closes the door behind her*)

JOAN. That was rather nice of you, George. You're beginning to think first. (*She sits on the sofa*)

GEORGE. I'm what?

JOAN. Never mind. So it's not the *Courier*.

STELLA. This is far worse. *The Daily Record.* You know what they're like.

JOAN. I should do. I worked for them for two years.

(STELLA *sits* R *of Joan on the sofa*)

GEORGE (*moving to* L *of the sofa*) So you did. (*He takes the card from Stella and studies it*) Do you know this fellow? "Thompson."

JOAN. Only by name. Used to work for the *Courier*. I suppose one of his pals there tipped him off. Why did he give the old lady his card? He must have known she'd show it to us.

GEORGE. What difference does it make? (*He crosses to the desk*) I'll have to tell Mr Elton.

JOAN. Not yet.

GEORGE. I must.

JOAN (*rising and moving to George*) Not yet. It's just a hunch. I may be wrong. And yet . . . George, will you let me handle this?

George. Joan, look . . .

Joan. What have you got to lose? If I'm wrong, you can still tell Mr Elton.

George. He ought to know now. Besides, what could you do?

Joan. It depends on whether they make the next move. I think they will.

George. Oh, they will—in print.

Joan. Have you got a better idea? (*She moves to the double doors*) Then let me try my way. Meanwhile, I'll go and have a word with Susan.

(Sarah *enters* l, *carrying an empty whisky bottle*)

Sarah. Who's been giving my Henry whisky?

Stella (*rising*) Oh, no!

Sarah. He's not supposed to have it.

George. Oh, Lord!

Sarah. You'd better come quick. I don't like the way he's breathing and I can't wake him up.

(Sarah *exits* l.
     Stella *follows her off*)

George (*to Joan*) Fetch Nurse. I'll ring for a doctor. (*He lifts the telephone receiver*)

(Joan *turns to go*)

And hurry. I came here to write his story—not his obituary. (*Into the telephone*) Hello . . . Hello . . .

Joan *exits by the double doors as—*
               the Curtain *falls*

Scene 2

Scene—*The same. About 7 p.m. the following evening.*

When the Curtain *rises, the lights are on and the window curtains are closed.* Joan *is seated at the desk, speaking on the telephone.*

Joan (*into the telephone*) Newsroom? . . . Yes, it is. Got a pencil? . . . Two more of Scott's victims have shown up . . . Yes, both women. Mrs Oxley, fourteen Arnley Street, Sheffield—widow, and Miss Felicity Bowes, aged fifty-seven, Signal Street, Dudley . . . Hold on . . .

(*The* Nurse *enters* l)

(*To the Nurse*) How is he, Nurse?

NURSE. Asleep. (*She crosses to* C) And he's not to be disturbed. The doctor insisted on complete rest.

JOAN. Yes, of course.

NURSE. I'm going to snatch a quick meal. (*She moves up* R) Call me at once if I'm needed.

JOAN. Very well, Nurse.

(*The* NURSE *exits by the double doors*)

(*Into the telephone*) Sorry. That was the nurse . . . Well, he'll not be able to come to the dinner but I reckon he'll survive, the tough old devil . . . Scott? . . . Remanded in custody . . . And was he surprised when they picked him up . . .

(BRENDA *enters by the double doors, wearing outdoor clothes. She moves* C)

I have to ring off. 'Bye. (*She replaces the receiver and rises. To Brenda*) Well, what a surprise.

BRENDA. Where is my husband?

JOAN. Dressing. (*She crosses to* R *of the sofa*) It's the concluding dinner tonight, thank God.

BRENDA (*indicating the door* R) In there?

JOAN. Yes.

BRENDA (*moving to the door* R) Thank you.

JOAN. George has been having rather a difficult time.

BRENDA. So?

JOAN. It would be a pity to add to his problems just now.

BRENDA. Thank you for telling me, Miss—Banstead, isn't it?

JOAN. That's right, Mrs Maxwell, if I'm not a little premature in calling you by that name.

(BRENDA, *about to knock on the door* R, *turns angrily, but says nothing. She changes her mind about knocking and opens the door*)

GEORGE (*off*) Brenda! Good Lord, you're back!

(BRENDA, *with a sneering glance at Joan, exits* R *and closes the door behind her*)

JOAN. Damn!

(HENRY *peers in at the door* L. *He is wearing pyjamas and dressing-gown. He hisses to Joan*)

(*She turns*) Mr Mellowes.

HENRY (*moving below the sofa*) Has that silly bitch of a nurse gone?

JOAN (*moving to* R *of Henry*) What are you doing out of bed? You know what the doctor said.

HENRY. That young fool!

JOAN. Back you go. Doctor's orders.

HENRY. Doctors! In my time I've had something like twenty different doctors and every blamed one of 'em is dead and I'm not. Where's my clothes?

JOAN. What do you want your clothes for?

HENRY. Damn it, I can't go to that there dinner like this.

JOAN. The dinner?

HENRY. I'm guest of honour, ain't I?

JOAN. Now listen . . .

HENRY. Not till I get my clothes.

JOAN. Mr Mellowes . . .

HENRY (*loudly*) Not till you gets my clothes.

JOAN. Now, be reasonable.

HENRY (*shouting*) Are you going to fetch my clothes or not?

JOAN. All right, all right. (*She goes to the desk*) But don't shout like that or you'll burst something. You're a sick man. (*She lifts the telephone receiver*)

HENRY (*moving* RC) Impertinence, that's what it is. A man ain't a man without his trousers.

JOAN (*into the telephone*) Valet service, please . . .

HENRY. Don't tell me they've gone and pressed 'em again.

JOAN (*into the telephone*) Oh, let me have the suit for Mr Mellowes, will you? . . . Thanks. (*She replaces the receiver*)

HENRY. If they press them trousers once more, the bloody things will start walking about by theirselves (*He sits in the armchair* C)

JOAN. Calm down. You're supposed to be taking things easy.

HENRY. Too much taking things easy around here.

JOAN. And you needn't think you're going to sit there.

HENRY. You mind your business and get me my clothes.

JOAN (*moving above the table* RC) They're coming, you mad, impatient thing, you. (*Gently*) How do you feel, Mr Mellowes? Honestly now.

HENRY. I reckon I'll live. Where's my missus?

JOAN. Downstairs, having her hair done.

HENRY. By a hairdresser?

JOAN. Why not? This is a big occasion for her.

HENRY. Must be fifty year or more since she had her hair done by a proper hairdresser. Dyed red, it was, too. Like some tart. By golly, did I give her a hiding.

JOAN (*sitting on the right arm of the sofa*) You're not giving her a hiding this time. You ought to be proud of her. She's a fine-looking woman.

HENRY. My Sarah?

JOAN. Yes, your Sarah.

HENRY. She were once. The years pass and you forget; but it's true; she were a beauty once. The men was all after her and she played hell with 'em. Specially me. She had long, thick, dark hair— right down below her backside, it were—and a sparkle in her eyes and rosy cheeks. She laughed a lot. A big hearty laugh it were, not this here silly giggling. And it made you laugh with her. Aye, all the men wanted her; but I wanted her most. I wanted her so much it hurt. Then she went off and married Bob Taylor. When I did finally get her it weren't the same. I wasn't right for her—not after Bob Taylor. I didn't really count. I never have.

Joan. I can't believe that.

Henry. It's human nature, I reckon. You get two men and a woman and you can bet she'll spurn the one as really wants her and throw herself at the one as doesn't care tuppence for her.

Joan (*with a glance at the door* R) How right you are.

Henry. No, I never counted with Sarah. Not proper like. Here, where's my suit?

Joan (*rising*) It's coming. You've very chatty tonight.

Henry. I been thinking, lying there. You can make a lot of mistakes in a hundred years. Reckon I made 'em all.

(Susan *enters by the double doors, carrying Henry's suit*)

Joan (*pointing* L) In there, please, Susan.

(Susan *crosses and exits* L)

Henry (*rising and crossing to* L) Reckon I'd better get ready for this here dinner.

Joan. I don't know if they'll let you go.

Henry. I'd like to see 'em stop me. I'm making a speech, ain't I? The one your Mr Elton wrote out for me.

Joan. Well, I'll speak to Mr Maxwell about it.

(Susan *enters* L *and stands aside for Henry*)

Henry. Give me a shout in about ten minutes, will you? Case I drops off. That's the worst of growing old. Takes you all your time to keep awake, let alone enjoy yourself.

(Henry *digs Susan in the ribs and exits* L. Susan *closes the door after him*)

Joan. Well, I don't know. (*She moves up* c) I hope it will be all right.

(Susan *crosses to the double doors*)

Susan. Susan, I'd like to talk to you.

Susan. Haven't you done me enough harm?

Joan. Susan, please.

Susan. You shopped him, you did. You got me to talk. You didn't say the police was after him. You got me to say where he was. Then you had him arrested.

Joan. But, Susan, you must see . . .

Susan. I don't want to talk about it.

(Susan *exits by the double doors.* Joan *takes a few steps after her, then stops with a shrug and moves up* c.
George *enters* R, *dressed in a dark suit*)

George (*as he enters; over his shoulder*) Yes, yes, I'll go down and fix you a place right away. (*He closes the door. To Joan*) She's—she's coming to the dinner.

Joan. Has she forgiven you for walking out on you?

George. One has to try to see her point of view.

Joan. Tell me, has she asked you to leave for her flat immediately after the dinner?

George. Well, yes, she has. Has he telephoned?

Joan. Thompson? No, not yet.

George. He won't. I shouldn't have listened to you.

Joan. There's time yet. Look, George, if you want something to worry about, go and see old Mr Mellowes. He's dressing himself for the dinner.

George (*moving to* R *of Joan*) But I thought he wasn't up to it.

Joan. He thinks differently. He's not only going, he's making his speech.

George. Oh, Lord! (*He crosses above the sofa*) I suppose I'd better have a word with him. What if something happens to him during the dinner?

Joan. Take it easy with him or, the mood he's in, something might happen to him right now. If I were you, I'd let him come.

George. I don't seem to have much choice.

Joan. George, will you be leaving for her flat?

George. I expect so.

Joan. Well, before you go, there's something I'd like to see you about.

George. Why not now?

Joan. Because . . .

(*The telephone rings*)

(*She crosses to the desk and lifts the receiver*) Let's hope it's Thompson this time. (*Into the telephone*) Penthouse suite . . . Yes, it is. Who's that? . . . I thought it might be . . .

George. Thompson?

(Joan *nods to George*)

Joan (*into the telephone*) Are you out of your mind? . . . Which bar are you in? . . . Well, stay there. (*She replaces the receiver*)

George. Well?

Joan (*moving to the double doors*) He'd like to be invited to the dinner so he can include it in the full story in Monday's *Record*.

George. Where is he?

Joan. American bar.

George (*crossing to her*) Well, it won't do any good, but at least I'll have the satisfaction of pushing his teeth down his throat.

Joan (*restraining George*) Oh, no, you won't. I'm handling this, remember?

George. Not any longer. This is my responsibility.

JOAN. Your responsibility is to see this story through without balling it up. And you won't do that by having a punch-up with Thompson. But there might be another way. I've a notion our friend Thompson might be persuaded to drop this story if the price is high enough.

GEORGE. I wish you were right.

JOAN. Perhaps I am.

GEORGE (*moving up* c) Anyway, where would I find that kind of money?

JOAN. You might ask your rich wife. (*She moves to* R *of George*) Anyhow, you stay right here and keep your fingers crossed.

(*Voices are heard off.*
STELLA *and* SARAH *enter by the double doors.* SARAH'S *hair has been stylishly remodelled*)

STELLA (*moving to the desk*) What do you think of her? Isn't she marvellous?

SARAH (*moving to* R *of Joan*) Get away with you!

JOAN. Your Henry's going to be proud of you.

SARAH. Him! He won't even notice I'm around.

STELLA (*to Joan*) How is he?

JOAN. Much better. Says he's coming to the dinner.

(JOAN *exits by the double doors*)

STELLA. Oh, but ought he to, after what the doctor said?

GEORGE (*moving to* L *of Sarah*) Perhaps you can talk sense into him?

SARAH. Me? I gave that up as hopeless long ago.

STELLA. Do you want any help in getting ready?

SARAH (*crossing to the door* L) No, dear. I can manage.

STELLA. Be sure to put on your new dress.

SARAH. Aye, that's going to make Henry's eyes pop. Especially if he thinks he's paying for it.

(SARAH *exits* L)

STELLA. I think it's done her good, bringing her here.

GEORGE (*moving and sitting on the sofa*) I'm glad it's done someone good.

STELLA (*moving to* R *of the sofa*) No, really, she's not been nearly so snappy today. It gave her quite a shock, Mr Mellowes not being well.

GEORGE. Me, too.

STELLA. It's time I went and got dressed.

GEORGE. Go ahead.

(ELTON *enters by the double doors. He wears a dark lounge suit*)

STELLA. I must fly. (*She moves to the double doors*) Excuse me, Mr Elton.

(STELLA *exits by the double doors*)

ELTON (*moving down* c) There must be a couple of hundred relations down there waiting to be fed. Family must have bred like rabbits. Well, any troubles?

GEORGE (*rising and moving down* L) No. None.

ELTON. Sure?

GEORGE. The old man's better. Coming to the dinner, after all.

ELTON. You sure they won't start another of their fights?

GEORGE. No. Not tonight.

ELTON. Something bothering you?

GEORGE. No. Nothing at all.

ELTON. Where's the old man?

GEORGE (*indicating the door* L) In there.

ELTON. Fetch him. If he's going to make his speech, I'd better rehearse it with him.

(GEORGE *crosses to the door* L *and knocks on it*)

You're keeping tabs on the Scott story, I hope?

GEORGE. You bet we are.

ELTON. I sensed he was a wrong 'un from the start. (*He moves down* R) I can smell them. I dare say I mentioned it to you.

GEORGE. Er—perhaps you did, sir. Matter of fact, he tried to swindle my wife. Wanted to sell her a share in some public relations business. She was telling me just now. (*He knocks on the door*)

ELTON. Just now?

GEORGE. Yes, sir. She's back. Coming to the dinner. I was just going to nip down and alter the table arrangements.

(HENRY *enters* L. *He is fully dressed*)

Oh, there you are.

HENRY. Well, young fellow, what is it?

GEORGE. Mr Elton would like a word with you.

HENRY. Who?

GEORGE. Our editor. You can't have forgotten him.

HENRY. Oh, ay, the stout fellow with the bad temper. Where is he?

ELTON. I'm here, thank you very much.

HENRY. Oh, so you are. (*He crosses to* c) Didn't see you standing there.

ELTON. So I gathered. I'm glad you're better.

HENRY. Nasty turn I had. I'm getting on, you know.

ELTON. Well, for that matter, so am I.

HENRY. Yes, you ain't wearing too well, are you? (*He moves to the armchair* c) You don't mind if I set myself down. The old legs don't seem to support me like they used to.

GEORGE (*crossing to the double doors*) I'll be off, then.

(GEORGE *exits by the double doors.* HENRY *sits laboriously in the armchair* c)

HENRY. Ah, that's a whole lot better, that is.

ELTON. You're quite comfortable?

HENRY. Aye. What can I do for you?

ELTON (*crossing above Henry to* L *of him*) I thought we might run over the speech you're to make, when I propose the toast this evening.

HENRY. That'd be the one you wrote out for me?

ELTON. Have you got it handy?

HENRY (*searching his sidepockets*) It's here somewheres. What's this here? (*He takes a slip of paper from his side pocket*)

ELTON (*taking the paper*) Let me see. (*He looks at the paper*) No, no, not this.

HENRY. You sure?

ELTON. Quite sure. It appears to be a piece of doggerel of doubtful propriety.

HENRY (*taking the paper and looking at it*) Ah, yes, the verger give me this. Pretty comical, isn't it? "A pretty young waitress named Teresa . . ."

ELTON. We haven't time for that. Here, allow me. (*He takes a paper from Henry's breast pocket*) This looks like it. (*He opens the paper and looks at it*) Yes, it is. (*He hands the paper to Henry*) Here, read it through with me, there's a good fellow.

HENRY. Right you are.

ELTON. You understand you speak after me. I'll call on you. That clear?

HENRY. I reckon so.

ELTON. Go ahead, then.

HENRY. I'd better stand up.

ELTON. Not now.

HENRY (*rising*) Can't be too careful with a job like this. 'Tisn't often as I makes a speech, you know.

ELTON. As you wish.

(HENRY *crosses below Elton to* L *of him, and clears his throat at length*)

Good God, man, do you have to do all that?

HENRY. All what?

ELTON. You're making a speech, not undergoing a medical examination. Oh, very well, get started.

(HENRY *studies the paper*)

Go on, man.

HENRY. Funny sort of typewriting, this.

ELTON. Damn it, you've got it upside down. (*He reverses the paper for Henry*) Now.

HENRY. Oh, ah, that makes quite a difference, don't it? Er—let

me see. Oh, yes. (*He reads*) "Mr Elton, ladies and gentlemen. I rise
to my feet . . ." (*He breaks off*)

ELTON. Go on.

HENRY. I been wondering about that bit.

ELTON. What bit?

HENRY. "I rise to my feet." I mean, they can see I'm not hanging
by my braces from the chandelier, can't they?

ELTON. It's a perfectly conventional opening. Oh, very well,
skip that and go on to the next line.

HENRY. Look, if you're going to be offended if I want it my
way . . .

ELTON. I'm not offended.

HENRY. I'm the one as got to make this speech.

ELTON. I'm well aware of that. (*He sits in the armchair* c) Do get
on with it.

HENRY (*reading*) "Mr Elton, ladies and gentlemen—for eighty
years I have never seen my wife . . ." (*He breathes deeply*)

ELTON. What? (*He rises and moves to* R *of Henry*) Show me. (*He
snatches the paper and looks at it*) No, no. "For eighty years I have never
seen my wife looking so happy."

HENRY (*snatching the paper*) That's what I was agoing to say.

ELTON. But you mustn't pause in the middle of it.

HENRY. I got to breathe.

ELTON. Breathe at the end of the sentence.

HENRY. I can't hold out that long.

ELTON. You can try.

HENRY. I'm doing me best.

ELTON (*moving* R) Oh!

HENRY (*reading*) "Mr Elton, ladies and gentlemen—for eighty
years I have never . . ." (*He gasps for want of breath*)

ELTON. Oh, my God!

HENRY. I has to breathe, I tell you. And I has to breathe my
way.

ELTON (*moving to* R *of Henry*) I don't care if you breathe once
every half minute through your left ear. Let's get this over. Start
there. (*He points*)

HENRY. This here?

ELTON. Yes, yes.

HENRY (*reading*) "Listening to Mr Elton pause for cheers."

ELTON. No, no, no, no!

HENRY. It says here . . .

ELTON. You pause for cheers. You don't say it. You pause while
they cheer.

HENRY. Oh, now I see.

ELTON. Good.

HENRY. Supposing they don't cheer? I'll look a proper ninny
standing there pausing . . .

ELTON. Of course they'll cheer. Do go on.

HENRY. I wasn't cut out for no speech-making.

ELTON. I agree with you. Fortunately, you won't have to make another for a hundred years. Go on.

HENRY (*reading*) "In his witty and moving speech, Mr Elton . . ." (*He breaks off*)

ELTON. Now what?

HENRY. Seems a lot about Mr Elton in my speech. This ain't your party, you know.

ELTON. I never said it was. Will you please continue?

HENRY. Mr Elton this—Mr Elton that. Seems to me it's all bloody Mr Elton.

ELTON. Heaven give me patience. Go on from there. (*He points*)

HENRY (*reading*) "He said my wife and I were the first—cenytenerarians . . ."

ELTON. No, no—"centenarians".

HENRY. That's what I said.

ELTON. You said "cenytenerarians".

HENRY. No, I didn't. I said "cenytenerarians".

ELTON. I know you did, but it should be "centenarians". (*He repeats slowly*) "Cen-ten-arians."

HENRY. Ah, now I see. "Cenytenerarians."

ELTON. No, no, you've got it wrong again. The word is "centenyarians". I mean, "cenateny—ceny—centienten . . ."

HENRY (*firmly*) "Cenytenerarians."

ELTON. No!

(GEORGE *enters by the double doors and moves up* C)

Thank God! (*He moves to* R *of George*) Another minute of him and I'd have been out of my mind. For heaven's sake, get him out of my sight.

HENRY. Here, just who do you think you're talking to?

ELTON (*moving down* R) Please!

HENRY. I didn't ask to be brought here, you know.

ELTON. All right, I apologize. I lost my temper. I'm sorry.

(GEORGE *moves to* L *of Henry*)

HENRY. So you should be. Man of your age. Serve you right if they did find out Sarah and me ain't married.

ELTON. What's he talking about now?

GEORGE. Nothing. (*To Henry*) Better run along and see how your wife's getting on.

HENRY. You tell him. See how he likes it.

ELTON. What is it he's burbling about?

HENRY. Reckons we could be sent to prison, don't you?

ELTON. Prison? Has he gone off his head or something?

GEORGE. Look, Mr Mellowes . . .

ELTON. Not married? Not married!

HENRY. No, we ain't.

ELTON. Of course they're married. They've got to be married.

GEORGE (*to Henry*) Did you have to blurt that out? Look, for Pete's sake, clear off for a minute, will you?

ELTON. You mean it's true?

GEORGE. I'll explain the whole thing in a moment.

ELTON. My God! (*He drops dazedly into the armchair* RC)

GEORGE. Mr Mellowes. (*He urges Henry to the door* L)

HENRY. All right, I'm going. He didn't ought to've talked to me like that. I never wanted to come here.

GEORGE. You told us.

HENRY. Had a lot to put up with, I have.

GEORGE. We'll talk about it later.

(HENRY *exits* L. GEORGE *closes the door after Henry then turns to face Elton*)

ELTON (*rising*) You idiot!

GEORGE. But they were married.

ELTON. Then what was he babbling about?

GEORGE. The old lady already had a husband living at the time.

ELTON. You don't mean—you can't mean they committed bigamy? (*He moves below the sofa*)

GEORGE. They didn't know it was bigamy.

ELTON. My God!

GEORGE. Perhaps I should explain.

ELTON. Explain! (*He sits on the sofa*) There are several hundred people down there. I'm making a speech, extolling the virtues of marriage and citing those two as the example of a lifetime.

GEORGE. Yes, sir, I know, but . . .

ELTON. As a reward for their marital fidelity, their commendable devotion, the *Gazette* is presenting them with their cottage. Why? So they may continue their bigamous liaison till they're a hundred and ten?

GEORGE. But, you see, sir . . .

ELTON. The leaders I've written. "The *Gazette* is for Marriage." I even had it on the posters. And one of those leaders was so nauseatingly sentimental that I was even affected myself and went home and kissed my wife for the first time in twenty years. I'll never live this down. Never!

GEORGE (*moving up* C) If it gets out. It may not. ————

ELTON (*rising*) *May* not? Does someone know?

GEORGE. Well . . .

ELTON. Do they?

GEORGE (*moving down* C) The *Daily Record*.

ELTON. What!

(ELTON *backs* GEORGE *down* R, *round the armchair* RC, *then up* C)

GEORGE. I'm afraid so, sir.

ELTON. Then we're finished. Finished.

GEORGE. Maybe not, sir. Joan's downstairs talking to him.

ELTON. Talking to who?

GEORGE. His name's "Thompson".

ELTON. Why the devil wasn't I told?

GEORGE. We hoped you wouldn't have to be.

ELTON. You damn fool! This'll be the end of me. I've got to act fast.

GEORGE. Look, sir . . .

ELTON. Shut up! I've got to think. (*He crosses down* L) The only hope is to get in before they do. That's it. We'll have this damn dinner but we won't have those two miscreants present.

GEORGE. Sir, if you'd only . . .

ELTON. When we've fed everybody and got them in a good mood, I'll make an announcement. I'll reveal how we've been fooled but how, at the last minute, through clever detective work, we unearthed the truth.

GEORGE. Expose them? (*He moves to* R *of Elton*) Before all their relations?

ELTON. You prefer the *Record* to expose them.

GEORGE. At least wait till Joan gets back. She thinks Thompson might be bought off.

ELTON. Not with my money he can't. And I'll tell you something else. You're fired.

GEORGE. All right, I'm fired. But I won't let you do this to them.

ELTON. Now, see here . . .

GEORGE. It's our fault they're in this mess. If we'd let them alone in their obscurity none of this would have come out. But no, we had to make a stunt of it. We had to bring them here, make a puppet show of them.

ELTON. And who started the whole thing off?

GEORGE. Not me.

ELTON. Damn it, you wrote them up in the first place.

GEORGE. Half a column. And that's where it should have stopped. Only you had to write a letter to the editor, pretending it came from a reader, suggesting we get up a fund to bring them here.

ELTON. I wrote no such letter. You're off your head.

GEORGE. It was typed on Stella's machine but not by her. I have it. If you take it out on the old people, I'll give it to the *Record* and they can complete the story.

ELTON. You wouldn't dare.

GEORGE. I mean it.

ELTON. Blast you!

GEORGE. I'm sorry. I get no pleasure out of doing this to you.

ELTON. What difference does it make if we expose them or the *Record* does it?

GEORGE. At least we'll come out of it with our hands clean.

ELTON. And our readers laughing us to scorn. I tell you one thing,

Maxwell, after this I'll see you never get another job on a paper as long as you live.

(JOAN *enters by the double doors*)

GEORGE. You can try.

JOAN (*moving to the armchair* RC *and sitting*) Well, well, it's quite like old times. Have you been fired again, George?

ELTON. Yes, he has. (*He crosses to* C) What happened downstairs?

JOAN. Give George his job back and I'll tell you.

ELTON. I'll do no such thing. This is blackmail.

JOAN. So it is. Well?

ELTON. He's sacked and he stays sacked.

JOAN. Is that your last word?

ELTON (*moving up* C) Yes, it is.

JOAN. Suit yourself.

ELTON. Now, you listen to me, young lady . . .

GEORGE (*crossing and standing above the table* RC) Joan, is there any hope?

JOAN. There might be, if we all behave ourselves.

ELTON. Don't you tell me to behave myself. (*He moves down* C) He's out, I tell you. And so will you be if you're not careful. Anyway, what's it to you? Anyone would think you're in love with the young fool. (*He moves down* L)

(GEORGE *turns and meets* JOAN's *gaze. She turns away*)

He's done this to me for the last time. Wait! Did you say there was hope of a way out?

JOAN. I did.

ELTON. Then out with it.

JOAN. And George?

ELTON (*after a struggle*) All right, damn you.

JOAN. Now, isn't that nice? We're all friends again.

GEORGE (*crossing down* R) Joan, for heaven's sake!

JOAN. Relax. My hunch was right. Every man has his price. Oh, not Thompson. In this matter Thompson is only a messenger-boy.

ELTON. What are you talking about? Out with it.

JOAN. He was here on behalf of his editor—John Brackley—you probably know him.

ELTON. I know him. A first-class skunk if ever there was one. (*He moves up* L)

JOAN. But clever. From the newsroom to the editor's desk in five years. Not bad, that. Of course, everybody hates his guts. And that includes me. I must have been mad when I married him.

ELTON. Brackley? (*He moves down* L) You married Brackley?

JOAN. Didn't I tell you? Well, it's been over for years. Except for the formalities. Now I'm letting him have the divorce he's been belly-aching about. So all is well. He won't print.

ELTON. Are you sure? Quite sure?

JOAN. The party can commence.

ELTON. I don't know what to say. (*He moves* C) I thought we were done for. (*To George*) And it's no thanks to you we're not. We'd better get this over before anything else happens. Hurry things along here. (*He moves to the double doors*) And if you think I'll forget your behaviour, Maxwell, you're wrong.

(ELTON *exits by the double doors*)

GEORGE (*crossing to* C) I don't know how to thank you.

JOAN. It's only a divorce. Besides, I may want to marry again myself one day.

GEORGE. He'll be a lucky man.

JOAN (*rising*) I expect you say that to all female press photographers.

GEORGE. It's funny. (*He moves to* L *of Joan*) I've never really got to know you till these last few days. It's as if you'd taken off a mask.

JOAN (*moving to the desk*) Well, we all wear one, don't we?

GEORGE. I don't know. I wish you hadn't.

JOAN. To tell you the truth, George, so do I.

(BRENDA *enters* R)

BRENDA. I hope I'm not interrupting anything important.

GEORGE (*moving up* RC) No, of course not.

BRENDA (*moving to* R *of George*) Are we ready for this entertainment—if that's the right word for it?

GEORGE. If you'd rather not come . . .

BRENDA. No, I must learn to do my duty. After all, I am your wife.

JOAN. Well, off and on.

(*The telephone rings*)

(*She lifts the receiver. Into the telephone*) Penthouse suite . . . Yes, Mr Elton . . . Yes, right away. (*She replaces the receiver. To George*) Forward, George. Mr Elton doesn't entirely care for the seating arrangements you've made.

GEORGE. He wouldn't. (*He moves to the double doors*) I suppose he'll find fault with everything I do from now onwards. Give Brenda a drink, will you, Joan? I shan't be five minutes. Oh, and you might rustle up the others. We ought to start soon.

(GEORGE *exits by the double doors.* JOAN *moves slowly to* L *of Brenda, then crosses above her to* R)

JOAN. What will you have?

BRENDA. Seeing the grisly time we're about to endure, I'd better have whisky.

JOAN. Certainly. (*She crosses to the bar and pours drinks*)

BRENDA (*moving above the sofa*) I had no idea George led this kind of life.

JOAN. He doesn't. This is one of our high spots of excitement.

BRENDA. Really?

JOAN. For him and for me. For instance, it's extremely rare for one of my pictures to lead to the arrest of a criminal. You heard about Scott, of course.

BRENDA. I read about it in the evening paper.

JOAN. Ah! (*She takes a drink and gives it to Brenda, then returns to the bar*)

BRENDA. I beg your pardon?

(JOAN *picks up her own drink, then sits on the bar stool, at the right end of it*)

JOAN. I merely said "Ah!" I was at Cannon Row Police Station when they arrested him. He tried so hard to bluff his way out of it.

BRENDA. I can imagine. He actually had the audacity to call at my flat last night with an offer of a partnership in some business for George. Naturally, I threw him out.

JOAN. Very wise of you. I wondered what he was doing at your flat.

BRENDA. You what?

JOAN. Susan told me he'd gone there. Oh, Susan is a chambermaid here. Like most women, she found Scott irresistible. Unfortunately, he now finds her easily resistible and the poor girl knows it.

BRENDA. Very interesting.

JOAN. Yes, isn't it? Rather sad, though, don't you think? Anyway, the jealous little fool watches him like a hawk and, having a cousin on the switchboard here, she usually gets to know what he's up to. I managed to persuade her to tell me where he'd gone. And, of course, I thought it my duty to inform the police.

BRENDA. Indeed! You could have thought of me. I might have had to give evidence or something if they'd arrested him at my place. Just imagine what people would have made of that.

(STELLA *enters by the double doors, dressed for the party*)

STELLA. What a rush! Oh, hello! I heard you were back. Aren't they ready yet?

JOAN. No sign of them.

STELLA. I'd better go and chase them. Maybe the old boy's fallen asleep.

(STELLA *crosses to the door* L, *taps on it, pauses, then exits* L)

JOAN (*rising and moving down* R) Where were we? Oh, yes, you were saying how unpleasant it would have been if the police had picked up Scott at your flat. I agree. George would have hated me for involving you. So I took precautions.

BRENDA (*moving down* C) I'm afraid I don't understand.

JOAN. I did a deal with the police. I refused to say where Scott was till they agreed to pick him up after he'd left your place. Well, they argued a bit but in the end they gave in. Such nice men. (*She moves* RC) You'd never have thought they were policemen.

BRENDA. Are you trying to tell me . . . ?

JOAN. They waited outside in their car. Mind you, they were a trifle put out having to wait until six-thirty this morning. But, as I told them, Scott was irresistible to women—well, to certain types of women.

BRENDA (*moving to* L *of Joan*) It's a lie. A filthy lie. If you've told this vile story to George . . .

JOAN. I haven't. He has enough on his mind just now. Still, I think he should know, don't you? I thought I'd tell him when this dinner's over.

BRENDA. You must be out of your mind.

JOAN. Think so? Then why have you returned so unexpectedly? Oh, you didn't know where Scott was picked up. True. But you feared he might have talked. So best to come and find out how much we know. And whip George away if you could. You might have got away with it, too. But you won't. I'll see to that.

BRENDA (*moving up* C) Lies. All lies. George won't believe a word of it.

JOAN. Then you've nothing to worry about—so long as you're confident George will accept your word rather than that of three policemen.

BRENDA. Why, you interfering little . . .

JOAN. Please! No compliments. (*She crosses down* L) I'll tell you something else. I'm no prude. In this game you can't be. But you disgust me. I enjoy doing this to you.

BRENDA. So you do. So you do. You hypocrite! You want him. You want him yourself.

JOAN. Could be.

BRENDA. You won't get away with this.

JOAN (*moving above the sofa*) We'll see. If I were you, I'd think up some excuse and steal quietly away.

BRENDA. Oh, no. I'll fight you. I'll fight you with everything I've got.

JOAN. You haven't got a lot (*She moves to* L *of Brenda*) Even for these days, it's a bit much to go through the ceremony with one man and the honeymoon with another.

BRENDA. You listen to me . . .

JOAN. Besides, he's not really your type. Far better call it a day.

BRENDA. I'll see you in hell first. (*She moves to the double doors*) And I've one important weapon left. He's in love with me.

JOAN. I'm beginning to wonder. Anyway, I'm sure he'll get over it in time. I'll do my best to help him. Matter of fact, I haven't been doing too badly already, in case you're interested.

BRENDA. I repeat: he's in love with me. That'll mean he'll want to believe me. And I'll think of something, never fear. And don't imagine I'll wait till you've poisoned his mind. I'll get in first.

Joan. Three policemen, remember—including the driver, of course.

(Stella *enters* L *and stands above the open door.*

Henry *and* Sarah, *dressed for the celebrations, enter* L. Henry *stands above the sofa.* Sarah *stands* L *of the sofa*)

Well!

Stella. Doesn't she look wonderful?

Joan. Marvellous!

Sarah. Maybe I don't look so bad, seeing I'm past my first girlish bloom.

Stella (*to Henry*) Aren't you proud of her?

Henry. I reckon she won't disgrace me.

Joan. We'll have you proposing marriage to her in a minute.

Henry. I might at that. Reckon I've had time to find out if we suit.

Sarah. Hark at the old fool! Tomorrow he'll be cursing me same as usual.

Stella. Oh, no.

Sarah. Yes, dear. But tonight I don't care. Tonight I've got a new dress and me hair done; and the long, long years don't seem so endless.

(George *enters by the double doors, leaving them open*)

George. Oh, good! We ought to be getting down.

Stella (*moving to* L. *of Henry*) Got your speech, Mr Mellowes?

Henry. Aye, but I'll let you into a secret. I'm not giving that one. I've writ one of me own. (*He moves up* C)

Joan. Thank heaven I have a seat near a door. (*She collects her camera from the table* L) Well, are we all ready? Stella?

Stella (*to Henry and Sarah*) You two first. Arm in arm, now.

Sarah (*moving to Henry*) Like this?

(Henry *and* Sarah *at first have some difficulty in linking arms*)

Stella (*moving above the sofa*) That's right.

Joan. Oh, George, your wife wants a word with you.

George (*moving above the table* RC) Now?

Joan (*to Brenda*) You did say now, didn't you, dear?

Brenda (*after some hesitation*) I have a headache. You'll have to go to your dinner without me.

George. But surely . . .

Brenda (*moving to the door* R) Please don't let's argue about it.

George. Brenda, just a moment . . .

Brenda. Oh, for God's sake, let me alone.

(Brenda *exits* R)

HENRY. By golly, just like our young days, eh, Sarah?

GEORGE (*moving to the door* R *and turning*) But I don't understand.

JOAN. You heard. She has a headache. But don't worry, I've a feeling it will be gone when we get back.

(HENRY *and* SARAH, *arm-in-arm, move to the double doors*)

(*She indicates Henry and Sarah*) Now, isn't that nice? And they lived happily ever after.

SARAH. It's just like our wedding day, eh, Henry!

HENRY. D'you have to remind me of that just when I'm beginning to enjoy myself?

(SARAH *gives an angry tug at his arm*)

HENRY. Not so fast, woman.

SARAH. Who's going fast?

(JOAN's *expression changes*)

HENRY. You are.

SARAH. I am not, you old fool.

HENRY. Dragging me along, you were.

HENRY *and* SARAH *exit by the double doors, grumbling, as—*

the CURTAIN *falls*

FURNITURE AND PROPERTY LIST

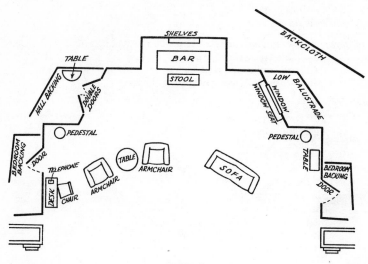

ACT I

On stage: Desk (down R) *On it:* telephone, inkstand, stationery rack with
  stationery, blotter
  Waste-paper basket
  Desk chair
  Pedestal (up R) *On it:* vase of flowers
  Armchair (RC)
  Table (RC) *On it:* ashtray
  Armchair (C)
  Sofa (LC) *On it:* cushions
  Table (L) *On it:* table-lamp, ashtray
  Pedestal (up L) *On it:* vase of flowers
  Bar (up C) *On it:* white cloth, assorted glasses and bottles includ-
  ing gin, whisky, sherry and vodka. 6 bottles beer, 6 bottles
  tonic water, 6 bottles ginger ale, syphon of soda, bottle opener,
  ashtray
  Shelves (behind bar) *On them:* glasses and bottles as dressing
  On wall over shelves: modern painting
  In front of bar: long stool
  On wall L: modern painting
  Carpet on floor

Window curtains
Light switch (L of double doors)
2 wall-brackets (R and L in alcove)
Built-in window-seat. *On it:* squab
In passage: console table. *On it:* vase of flowers

Doors closed
Window curtains open
Light fittings off

Off stage: Brief-case. *In it:* notebook, pencil (STELLA)
Portable typewriter (STELLA)
Camera and flash (JOAN)
Brief-case. *In it:* copy of speech (ELTON)

Personal: GEORGE: coin
BRENDA: handbag
HENRY: stick
SARAH: spectacles

ACT II

Strike: Flowers on pedestals
Dirty glasses
Stella's hat and coat
Elton's hat, coat and brief-case
Speech from floor

Set: *On desk:* 3 copies of broadcast
On sofa: Joan's camera with film to change
Behind R cushion: Nurse's knitting

Doors closed
Window curtains open
Light fittings off

Off stage: 2 vases of flowers (SCOTT)
Henry's suit (SUSAN)
Tray. *On it:* 2 bottles of medicine, 2 glasses, 2 spoons (NURSE)
Battery-operated tape-recorder (GEOFFREY)

Personal: HENRY: stick
SARAH: handkerchief
GEOFFREY: handkerchief

ACT III

SCENE I

Strike: Whisky bottle from bar
Camera
Knitting

Set: On table RC: newspaper with photograph of crowd on front page
Doors closed
Window curtains closed
Light fittings on

Off stage: Bottle of pills (SUSAN)
Visiting card (SARAH)
Empty whisky bottle (SARAH)

SCENE 2

Strike: Dirty glasses

Set: Clean glasses
On desk: notebook
On bar: full bottle of whisky
On table L: Joan's camera
Doors closed
Window curtains closed
Light fittings on

Off stage: Henry's suit (SUSAN)

Personal: HENRY: slip of paper in side pocket, copy of speech in breast
pocket

LIGHTING PLOT

Property fittings required: 3 wall-brackets, table-lamp
Interior. A sitting-room. The same scene throughout
THE APPARENT SOURCES OF LIGHT are, in daytime, a window up LC;
and at night, wall-brackets up RC and up LC, and a table-lamp L
THE MAIN ACTING AREAS are RC, up C, down C and LC

ACT I. Early afternoon in spring
To open: Effect of spring sunshine
Fittings off
No cues

ACT II. Morning
To open: Effect of spring sunshine
Fittings off
No cues

ACT III, SCENE 1. Evening
To open: Fittings on
No cues

ACT III, SCENE 2. Evening
To open: Fittings on
No cues

EFFECTS PLOT

ACT I

Cue 1   JOAN: ". . . hot cocoa each."   (Page 10)
           Telephone rings

Cue 2   ELTON: ". . . even about that."   (Page 13)
           Telephone rings

Cue 3   ELTON: ". . . over the place."   (Page 22)
           Telephone rings

Cue 4   BRENDA: "George!"   (Page 24)
           Telephone rings

ACT II

Cue 5   SCOTT: ". . . her for you."   (Page 29)
           Telephone rings

Cue 6   JOAN: ". . . moment around here."   (Page 31)
           Glass crash off L

ACT III

SCENE 1

Cue 7   After rise of CURTAIN   (Page 46)
           Telephone rings

SCENE 2

Cue 8   JOAN: "Because . . ."   (Page 59)
           Telephone rings

Cue 9   JOAN: "Well, off and on."   (Page 68)
           Telephone rings

Character costumes and wigs used in the performance of plays contained in French's Acting Edition may be obtained from Messrs CHARLES H. FOX LTD, 184 High Holborn, London W.C.1.